# The Art of
# Romanian
## Cooking

# The **Art** of Romanian Cooking

## Galia Sperber

**PELICAN PUBLISHING COMPANY**
Gretna 2002

The word "Pelican" and the depiction of a pelican are trademarks
of Pelican Publishing Company, Inc., and are registered
in the U.S. Patent and Trademark Office.

**Library of Congress Cataloging-in-Publication Data**

Sperber, Galia.
    The art of Romanian cooking / Galia Sperber.
       p. cm.
    Includes index.
    ISBN 1-56554-929-5 (alk. paper)
     1. Cookery, Romanian. I. Title.

TX723.5.R8 S64 2002
641.59498—dc21

2002016963

Printed in the United States of America
Published by Pelican Publishing Company, Inc.
1000 Burmaster Street, Gretna, Louisiana 70053

*To my mother, Miriam,
and to the loving memories of my grandmother Fanny
and my great-grandmother Sally—the three pillars on
which my existence stands*

# Contents

# ABBREVIATIONS

### STANDARD

| tsp. | = | teaspoon |
| tbsp. | = | tablespoon |
| oz. | = | ounce |
| qt. | = | quart |
| lb. | = | pound |

### METRIC

| ml. | = | milliliter |
| l. | = | liter |
| g. | = | gram |
| kg. | = | kilogram |
| mg. | = | milligram |

## STANDARD-METRIC APPROXIMATIONS

| $\frac{1}{8}$ teaspoon | = | .6 milliliter | | |
| $\frac{1}{4}$ teaspoon | = | 1.2 milliliters | | |
| $\frac{1}{2}$ teaspoon | = | 2.5 milliliters | | |
| 1 teaspoon | = | 5 milliliters | | |
| 1 tablespoon | = | 15 milliliters | | |
| 4 tablespoons | = | $\frac{1}{4}$ cup | = | 60 milliliters |
| 8 tablespoons | = | $\frac{1}{2}$ cup | = | 118 milliliters |
| 16 tablespoons | = | 1 cup | = | 236 milliliters |
| 2 cups | = | 473 milliliters | | |
| $2\frac{1}{2}$ cups | = | 563 milliliters | | |
| 4 cups | = | 946 milliliters | | |
| 1 quart | = | 4 cups | = | .94 liter |

## SOLID MEASUREMENTS

| $\frac{1}{2}$ ounce | = | 15 grams | | |
| 1 ounce | = | 25 grams | | |
| 4 ounces | = | 110 grams | | |
| 16 ounces | = | 1 pound | = | 454 grams |

# Acknowledgments

My interest in cookery started early on in my life, but when I started to write this book, I never imagined the task that awaited me, having to detail how to produce every dish. Though I have to thank my late grandmother for doing the hard work—keeping an extensive recipe book—its translation from Romanian and adaptation to modern cooking was nevertheless something that kept me busy for over a year. I could not have done this work without the invaluable advice and support of both my parents, Miriam and Charles Sperber. Their memories of the tastes and smells of Romanian cooking are far more reliable and accurate than my own, and their enthusiasm and encouragement for this project are what drove me to complete it. I would also like to thank my brothers, Steve and Alex, for being my chief tasters over the years and never being afraid to tell me when I got it wrong. Finally, I would like to thank my fiancé, Eldad Avital, for becoming the latest addition to my tasters, and for supporting me in this literary and culinary adventure.

# Introduction

Old family documents show that my mother's family lived in the green fields of northern Romania beginning in the 1500s. Fortunately, when my grandparents emigrated to the West in the 1960s, none of the old traditions were lost, and I was lucky enough to get a taste of this wonderful past.

My earliest memories of my grandmother's home have very vivid smells attached to them—little chocolate treats made with rum in pretty paper cupcake holders and white fish in a mouthwatering tomato sauce. Until about the age of six I spent most of this visiting time running through the rooms of the house, occasionally stopping to watch what was going on in the kitchen. I remember the time when my great-grandmother finally allowed me to help by grating some potatoes for her—a triumph of maturity for me—and cutting my finger five minutes into the task.

My interest in cooking started in Grandma's kitchen and by the age of seven I was making some easy dishes for my family (with the help of a chair, on which I stood to reach the kitchen counter more easily). To my great regret, my grandmother passed away much too early for me to have learned all her culinary secrets, but her recipes and the time we spent cooking together remain deeply cherished in my heart.

Romania lies in the center of Eastern Europe and has borders with the Ukraine, Moldova, Bulgaria, Serbia, Hungary, and the Black Sea. These boundaries were set in 1918, but previously the area was loosely held together by occupation by various nations. Political changes and the influx of peoples over the centuries have resulted in a rich mix of cultural influences in Romania. This is evident in the country's architecture, culture, and cuisine.

The first united community in the region of Romania arose before the first century B.C. with the Dacian Kingdom. Dacia was centered in the mountains of southern Transylvania. The kingdom flourished until the first century A.D., when it was conquered by the Roman armies led by Emperor Trajan. The resulting Daco-Roman population adopted the Latin language and culture and accepted the Christian religion.

In A.D. 271 the Romans withdrew from all territories north of the Danube, but the Daco-Romans remained a united community, despite the centuries of invasions that followed. The Romanian language developed and the Christian Church was founded during the period of influence of the Orthodox Byzantine Empire.

At this stage, three feudal states emerged: Transylvania, Moldavia, and Wallachia. Together they fought to keep the Ottoman Empire out of Romania, but as this became more difficult the three principalities were forced to come under Turkish sovereignty, although they were never occupied.

The next big crisis in Romanian history occurred in the 18th century, when the principalities were caught in the middle of struggles among the Austrian, Russian, and Ottoman empires. This resulted in chunks of the area coming under separate rule by each of these empires. In 1918 Transylvania united with Romania to form the Romanian Kingdom, with its boundaries as they are today.

This summarized history of the country illustrates the origins of the cultural diversity apparent today in Romania. Slavic, Latin, and Balkan influences helped develop food that sometimes retained its origin and other times became totally Romanian. Polenta is very characteristically Romanian (*mămăligă*), but it is also found in Italian cookery. Another example is traditional Turkish fare such as stuffed grape leaves, which have been adopted into Romanian cuisine.

The landscape of the country also allowed for a rich and varied diet. Romania is made up of mountainous terrains in the north and center, the Carpathian Mountains. Around them, the land is covered by hills and tablelands, which are well suited for orchards and vineyards. Fertile plains cover the rest of the country, where grains, vegetables, herbs, and other crops are grown.

A lot of care and devotion was traditionally given to cooking in Romania, and the meals that were prepared were always meant for sharing. Women cooking together to prepare a multitude of delicacies was a common sight in past times. Families were large and united and would seldom eat separately. This made the dining table a center of social interaction that often attracted numerous guests. The pride of a household was its ability to please those they served with foods of excellent quality and endless variety. That is why none of my grandmother's recipes are in small quantities and I have made them all to serve six.

I have tried to keep the instructions and ingredients for each recipe as uncomplicated as possible. This was in fact an easy task, because in the past most dishes were produced from memory and naturally it was necessary to keep things simple. I hope that both those with culinary curiosity alone as well as avid cooks will enjoy using the recipes of the wonderful Romanian cuisine and eating the food on which my ancestors were raised.

# The Art of
# Romanian
## Cooking

# Appetizers

Romanian hospitality revolves around the table. As a child you quickly learn the routine, and when visiting another Romanian home you know that arriving with an empty belly is a good thing. "How are you?" is quickly followed by "What can I get you to eat?" So many of the simplest and most delicious Romanian recipes are served as snacks or starters that a feast can result just by laying out a combination of these.

My grandmother was happiest when entertaining and, together with my great-grandmother, loved to present the best fare possible. My mother remembers that she did this with an apparent effortlessness that was amazing. Guests visiting my grandmother's home always knew they were guaranteed a satisfying meal.

The following recipes are meal starters or can be served several at a time for light summer lunches. The first ones are exemplary of the Romanian practice of stuffing. Tomatoes and peppers are most commonly stuffed with flavored mixtures, either vegetarian or containing meat, but eggs, courgettes (zucchini), cabbage, and grape leaves are also used.

# AUBERGINE-STUFFED TOMATOES
## (roşii umplute cu vinete)

1 large aubergine (eggplant)
3 tbsp. vegetable oil
2 onions (finely chopped)
2 tbsp. chopped parsley
Salt
Pepper
12 small round tomatoes (very firm)
12 sprigs parsley

Wrap the aubergine in aluminum foil and bake at 400 degrees (200 degrees C) until it feels soft inside the foil (about 45 minutes). Remove the foil and peel off the skin. Chop up the soft flesh and transfer to a bowl. Mix the chopped aubergine with the oil, onions, chopped parsley, and salt and pepper to taste, until the mixture is smooth. Cut off the top of each tomato. With a small spoon, remove all the tomato seeds. Fill the tomatoes with the aubergine mixture and decorate each with a sprig of parsley. Serve on a mixed-leaf salad.

# CHEESE-STUFFED PEPPERS
## (ardei umpluţi cu brînză)

6 large green bell peppers
2 cups / 500 g. ricotta or cottage cheese
⅓ cup / 100 g. butter or margarine
1 tbsp. chopped chives
1 tbsp. chopped dill

Cut the tops off the peppers and clean out the seeds, then set aside. Beat together the cheese and butter, then add the chives. Fill each pepper with the cheese mixture and top with a bit of dill. Serve with toasted French bread slices.

# EGGS FILLED WITH FISH PASTE
## (ouă umplute cu paste de peşte)

6 eggs
1 tbsp. olive oil
2 tbsp. fish paste
1 tbsp. mustard
Shredded lettuce
White-wine vinegar
Olive oil
12 green olives (pitted)

Hard-boil the eggs and allow them to cool. Remove the shells and cut each egg in half lengthwise. Carefully remove the yolks and transfer to a bowl. Mix these with 1 tbsp. oil until smooth, then fold in the fish paste and mustard. (For the fish paste, use either a bought paste or see the recipe for herring and nut spread at the end of this chapter.) Arrange the egg halves on a bed of shredded lettuce sprinkled with a few drops of vinegar and olive oil. Decorate each egg half with half an olive.

# EGGS FILLED WITH SOUR CREAM AND SAUCE
## (ouă umplute cu sos de smăntîna)

**6 eggs**
**1 small onion (minced)**
**1 tbsp. butter**
**2 tbsp. sour cream**
**Salt**
**Pepper**
**1 tbsp. vegetable oil**
**12 slices (1¾ inch / 12 x 2 cm.) French bread**
    **(soaked in milk)**

Hard-boil the eggs (about 6 minutes) and allow them to cool. Remove the shells and cut each egg in half lengthwise. Carefully remove the yolks and transfer to a bowl. Fry the onion until soft but without browning, then add the cooled fried onion and the butter to the cooked egg yolks. Mix until they form a smooth paste, fold in the sour cream, and add salt and pepper to taste. Fill the egg halves with the mixture. In a pan containing the oil, fry the slices of bread until they become golden brown. Remove from the pan and cut out just enough of the center of each slice to allow each egg half to rest in the bread without tipping over.

**SAUCE**
**1 tbsp. butter (melted)**
**1 tbsp. flour**
**1 cup / 250 ml. vegetable stock**
**2 egg yolks**
**2 tbsp. milk**
**1 tbsp. chopped dill**
**Salt**
**Fresh parsley (chopped)**

To make the sauce, mix the butter and flour in a saucepan and allow to come to the boil. Then add the stock and simmer for 5 minutes. Remove from the heat and stir in the egg yolks, milk, dill, and salt to taste. Place the prepared bread slices on a presentation plate, drizzle sauce over them, and sprinkle with parsley.

## BAKED FILLED BREAD ROLLS
### (chifle umplute)

For any child who grows up with a working mother, the weekends are greatly anticipated. This is a time when I would wake up and find my mother dressed casually, looking relaxed, chatting, and making breakfast with my grandmother. One of the best weekend treats would be *frigănele*, or what is also known as French toast—slices of white bread soaked in milk, dipped in egg yolk, fried lightly in butter, then served with sugar sprinkled on top. The smell of the frying bread was enough to guarantee that the day got off to a good start.

This recipe is for another dish that we sometimes had on these lazy weekend mornings.

> 6 small bread rolls
> 1¼ cups / 300 ml. milk
> ⅔ cup / 150 g. ricotta cheese
> 1 egg
> Pinch salt
> 1 tsp. chopped dill
> 1 tsp. chopped chives
> ½ tsp. chopped oregano
> ⅓ cup / 100 g. butter or margarine
> ⅓ cup / 100 ml. sour cream

Cut the bread rolls in half (like sandwiches) and dip them in a shallow bowl of milk until they are soaked through to the crust. In another bowl, mix the cheese with the egg, salt, dill, chives, and oregano. Cover each half-roll with the mixture, then top with another half-roll.

Cut the butter into 12 equal pieces. Place 6 pieces in a casserole, put each roll on top of one of the pieces of butter, then place another piece of butter on top of each roll. Now cover each roll with a good tablespoon of sour cream. Bake at 400 degrees (200 degrees C) for 20-30 minutes. Serve hot.

## MOSAIC BREAD
### (pîine mozaic)

¼ lb. / 125 g. sardines
½ loaf French bread
Few tbsp. milk
⅔ cup / 150 g. butter or margarine
¼ lb. / 125 g. Emmenthaler or Swiss cheese
½ pickled red pepper (see Peppers Pickled in Vinegar)
10 black olives

In a food processor, mix the sardines, a handful of bread hollowed out from the baguette and soaked in milk, and the butter until it becomes smooth and pasty. Cut the cheese and pepper into small cubes and fold into the paste. Refrigerate the mixture. Hollow out the rest of the baguette until only about ⅓ inch (1 cm.) thickness is left inside. With a spoon, fill the crust with the cooled mixture. Refrigerate again. Serve when set by cutting ⅓-inch (1-cm.) slices. Serve with black olives. This can be prepared several days in advance.

# VEGETABLE-STUFFED BREAD CUPS
## (cupe de franzelă umplute cu legume)

1½ tbsp. butter
8 oz. / 250 g. French bread (cut into 6 slices)
1 large potato
8 oz. / 250 g. peas (canned or frozen)
Salt
3 tbsp. chopped parsley
Pepper
4 tbsp. shredded Swiss or cheddar cheese

Melt 1 tbsp. of the butter in a pan, then add the bread slices and fry on one side only until golden brown. Fit each slice into a small ovenproof bowl, forming cups with the bread. Boil the potato until cooked but still holding its shape. Cool, peel, and cut into thin slices. Warm the peas in a pan, in the remaining butter. Assemble the dish by first covering the bottom of each cup with potato slices. Season with salt, parsley, and pepper. Next add some peas and cover with shredded cheese. Bake at 350 degrees (180 degrees C) for 15-20 minutes, until warmed through and the cheese has melted over the vegetables. Serve hot.

# BASKETS FILLED WITH "BOEUF SALAD"
## (coşulete umplute cu salată de boeuf)

Salată de boeuf is one of those recipes that is useful when meat is left over from a big meal. In my family, when we have roast chicken or a big beef roast, this will be on the menu for the next day. These days my father is the specialist—it's his job to have this ready for anyone who gets hungry. Sometimes we have it as a salad on its own, but the baskets are a nicer way of presenting it as a starter.

4-5 small potatoes (boiled and cold)
1 carrot (boiled and cold)
5 celery stalks
2 pickles
½ lb. / 250 g. cooked boneless chicken or beef
   (cold)
Chopped parsley
2 oz. / 50 g. canned peas
1 cup / 250 ml. mayonnaise
2 tsp. mustard

Make the salad by cutting the potatoes, carrot, celery, pickles, and meat into small cubes. Place in a large bowl and add the parsley and peas. Blend the 1 cup mayonnaise and the mustard in a small bowl, then add it to the vegetables and meat until they are all coated.

**BASKETS**
1 egg
1 cup / 250 g. butter or vegetable oil
Salt
2 cups / 500 g. flour
Mayonnaise
Olives

To make the baskets, whisk the egg and butter or oil together in a bowl. Add the salt and flour, and mix until a smooth dough is formed. Divide the dough into balls of 2 inches (5 cm.) diameter and roll out into sheets ⅓ inch (1 cm.) thick. Place each sheet in a greased tartlet dish, cut off excess dough, and prick the base a few times with a fork. Bake at 350 degrees (180 degrees C) until the tartlets are firm and golden brown (10-15 minutes). Allow to cool completely and fill with the salad. Top with a dollop of mayonnaise and an olive. The salad and baskets can be made separately days ahead and assembled just before serving.

# STUFFED GRAPE LEAVES
## (sarmale cu foi de viţă)

This recipe clearly shows the influence of Turkey and Greece on Romanian culture. A similar recipe known as dolmas in Greek cuisine is as common there as it is in Romania.

> 25-30 grape leaves
> 1 small onion (chopped)
> 1 tbsp. white rice
> 4 tbsp. water
> 1 lb. / 500 g. lamb (minced)
> ½ tbsp. chopped parsley
> Salt
> Pepper
> 3 tomatoes
> 1 small can tomato paste

Wash the grape leaves and drain. In a saucepan, brown the onion and rice, then add water, cover, and simmer until the rice absorbs all the water. In a bowl, mix the rice, meat, parsley, and seasonings. Take 1 tbsp. of mixture and place in the center of a grape leaf, then roll (folding in the edges) to form a small sausage. In a pot, place a layer of sliced tomato. Add the stuffed grape leaves and finish with tomato slices. Dilute the tomato paste in water 3 times its volume and pour into the pot. Cover the pot and simmer on a small flame about 45 minutes.

# SALAMI CROQUETTES
## (crochete din salam)

---

6 tbsp. butter
⅔ cup / 150 g. flour
1½ cups / 350 ml. water
4 eggs
1 tsp. salt
5 oz. / 150 g. salami (chopped)
4 tbsp. fine breadcrumbs

Melt 3 tbsp. butter in a saucepan. Dissolve the flour in the water and add to pan. Simmer and keep mixing to prevent lumps. After the sauce has thickened sufficiently, remove from heat and allow to cool. Add 3 eggs, the salt, and salami and mix well. With moist hands, shape handfuls into croquettes. Next roll the croquettes in a beaten egg and then in breadcrumbs. Fry in the remaining butter until golden brown.

### TARTAR SAUCE
2 eggs
3 green onions
3 tbsp. chopped parsley
1⅗ cups / 400 g. mayonnaise
3 tbsp. mustard
Salt
1 tsp. pepper

To make the sauce, hard-boil the eggs, then cool and cut into a fine dice, along with the green onions and parsley. Mix with the mayonnaise, mustard, and seasonings, until it is all smooth and creamy.

# MUSHROOM AND FISH CROQUETTES
## (crochete din ciuperci cu peşte)

½ lb. / 250 g. button mushrooms
Salted water
1 lb. / 500 g. fish fillet (any white fish)
1 onion (chopped)
3 tbsp. vegetable oil
2 slices white bread (soaked in milk with crusts
    removed)
2 eggs
3 tbsp. flour
2 tbsp. chopped parsley
2 tbsp. chopped dill
½ tsp. pepper
1 tsp. salt

Chop the mushrooms and bring to the boil in salted water. Drain and cool. Cut the fish fillet into small pieces. Fry the onion in 1 tbsp. oil until soft, then add the mushrooms, fish, and softened bread. Allow to cool, then add 1 egg, 1 tbsp. flour, and the herbs and seasonings. Shape the mixture into croquettes, roll through the remaining flour, dip in beaten eggs, then in flour again. Fry in hot oil. Serve with a tomato sauce.

# MUSHROOM GELATIN WITH MAYONNAISE
## (ciuperci cu gelatină si maioneză)

**2 lb. / 1 kg. button mushrooms**
**1 onion (sliced into rings)**
**2 cloves garlic (minced)**
**Pinch salt**
**Pinch pepper**
**Water to cover**
**1 tsp. butter**
**Gelatin sheets**
**Water for gelatin**
**Mayonnaise**
**Chopped chives and parsley**

Clean and cut the mushrooms into thin slices. Place in a deep pan and add the onion rings, garlic, salt, pepper, and butter. Cover with water and bring to the boil. Simmer on medium heat for 10 minutes. Remove the pan from the heat and drain the mushrooms, reserving the cooking liquid in a saucepan. Discard the onion and garlic. Soak the gelatin sheets in cold water to soften them, then add them to the liquid (3 sheets per 1 cup / 250 ml. liquid). Heat the saucepan and keep stirring until the gelatin is completely dissolved. Divide the mushrooms into 6 small soufflé dishes and top with the liquid. Refrigerate until set. When ready to serve, turn the dishes onto plates and serve with a dollop of mayonnaise and a sprinkling of chives and parsley. (A trick for getting the gelatin to slide out in one nice piece is to dip the soufflé dish into a bowl of hot water for a second or two and then turn it onto a plate.)

# EGG CROQUETTES WITH TARTAR SAUCE
## (crochete din ou cu sos tartar)

**6 eggs**
**1 cup / 250 g. flour**
**1⅓ cups / 400 ml. milk**
**2 tbsp. butter**
**Pinch salt**
**1 tsp. pepper**
**¾ cup / 200 g. breadcrumbs**
**⅓ cup / 100 ml. vegetable oil**

Hard-boil 4 of the eggs and cut into thick slices. In a bowl, mix the flour and milk. Melt the butter in a saucepan and add the flour mixture. Bring to the boil then remove from heat and allow to cool. Next mix in 1 raw egg, salt, and pepper. Now fold in the hard-boiled eggs. Crack the remaining egg into a plate and beat. Using wet hands, take large spoonfuls of the egg and flour mixture and shape to form thick sticks. Roll in the beaten egg and then in the breadcrumbs to coat. Heat the oil in a pan and fry the croquettes until they are golden brown and firm. Serve cold with tartar sauce (see Salami Croquettes recipe).

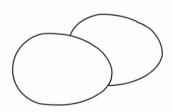

# EGG ROULADE WITH SPINACH
## (ruladă din omleta cu spanac)

½ lb. / 250 g. large tomatoes
2¼ lb. / 1.2 kg. spinach
Pinch salt
1 tsp. pepper
4 eggs
4 tbsp. butter
½ tsp. salt
1 tbsp. melted butter
4 oz. / 100 g. fried onions
⅓ cup / 100 ml. sour cream

Cut the tomatoes into thin slices. Cook the spinach by boiling in salt water for 10 minutes. Drain, rinse in cold water, and chop coarsely. Transfer the spinach to a bowl, add pinch salt and the pepper, and toss. In a fresh bowl, beat the eggs with the 4 tbsp. butter and ½ tsp. salt. Pour into a large hot pan containing 1 tbsp. melted butter and cook the eggs until they set and form a thin omelette. Remove the omelette and cut in half. On one half spread a tablespoon of the spinach, then a layer of fried onions, then another layer of spinach. Roll the omelette in a clean towel and wrap in plastic wrap. Repeat with the second half. Refrigerate for at least 1 hour. Remove from plastic wrap and cut into ¼-inch (½-cm.) slices. Serve each roll on a slice of tomato with sour cream.

# EGGS WITH LEEKS
## (ochiuri cu praz)

3 leeks
4 tbsp. butter
1 tbsp. flour
1 cup / 250 ml. milk
1 tbsp. white-wine vinegar
6 eggs
6 thick slices white bread (toasted)
Grated parmesan cheese
Salt

Cut away the green parts of the leeks. Slice the white parts into thin rings. Next melt the butter in a frying pan, add the flour, and mix. Add the milk. Simmer for about 5 minutes, then add the sliced leeks. Fry for 5 minutes and remove from heat. To prepare the eggs, boil water in a wide pot. Add vinegar. Break the eggs individually in a glass, then carefully allow each to slide out into the boiling water. When all the eggs are in the water, cover the pot and simmer on a low flame about 3 minutes. Then remove each egg using a slotted spoon and lay carefully on a plate. Butter a casserole, then lay the bread slices in a layer. Next lay an egg on each slice. Pour the leek sauce over the eggs, sprinkle with parmesan and salt, and bake at 450 degrees (240 degrees C) just until the cheese begins to melt, about 5 minutes.

# CHEESE ROLLS
## (rulou cu pastă de brînză)

This recipe is traditionally made with a mountain cheese called *caşcaval* (caschcaval), light yellow, semihard, and with a distinct flavor close to that of the Italian cheese provolone, which is what my grandmother used in this recipe after she left Romania. These days, it may be possible to find the real caschcaval in specialty shops that import Eastern European foods.

> 5 oz. / 150 g. butter
> 5 oz. / 150 g. margarine
> 1⅓ cups / 350 g. flour
> 1 tsp. salt
> 5 tbsp. vinegar
> 2 tbsp. water
> 1 egg (beaten)

Blend the butter and margarine until smooth. Shape into a ball and set aside in the refrigerator for 20 minutes. Meanwhile, pour most of the flour (reserve a few tablespoons) onto a board and make a well in the center. Into the well put the salt, vinegar, and water. Work into the flour to form a dough, adding water if necessary. Form into a ball and refrigerate for 20 minutes.

Next sprinkle the remaining flour onto a board and roll out the dough into a thin square. Put the butter and margarine mixture in the center, and bring the corners of the dough up to close the filling in. Roll again, this time leaving the dough flat but thicker, and refrigerate again for 30 minutes. Bring the dough out, roll and fold in 4, refrigerate 30 minutes again, and repeat twice more. Roll out the pastry, then cut into strips of 1x4 inches (10x2 cm.), brush the edges with beaten egg, and roll each up, forming a tube. Bake at 350 degrees (180 degrees C) for 20 minutes, then leave to cool.

**FILLING**
10 oz. / 300 g. caschcaval or provolone cheese
¾ cup / 200 g. butter
10 oz. / 300 g. soft goat cheese
2 tsp. paprika

To make the filling, shred the cheese, then beat with the butter. Now add the goat cheese and paprika and mix well. Put mixture into piping bag with a thick nozzle and fill the rolls. Refrigerate until ready to serve.

## SAVORY FRIED CHEESE PATTIES
(papanaşi prăjiţi)

8 oz. / 250 g. ricotta cheese
4 eggs (separated)
4 tbsp. flour
2 tbsp. minced chives
1 tsp. salt
½ tsp. pepper
2 tbsp. butter

In a bowl, beat together the cheese, egg yolks, flour, chives, salt, and pepper. Beat the whites separately until stiff, then fold into the cheese mixture. Using wet hands, shape spoonfuls of the mix into balls the size of apricots, then flatten them into patties. Fry in hot butter until lightly golden. Serve hot.

# BREADED CASCHCAVAL
## (caşcaval pané)

½ cup / 100 ml. flour
1 egg (beaten)
½ cup / 100 ml. breadcrumbs
Pat butter
6 thick slices caschcaval or provolone cheese
½ lemon (sliced)

Place the flour, egg, and breadcrumbs in 3 separate dishes. Preheat a large frying pan containing butter. Flour each slice of cheese, then dip in the egg, then coat with breadcrumbs. Fry on both sides until golden brown and serve immediately or cold, with slices of lemon.

# PEAS ON FRIED BREAD
## (frigănele cu mazăre)

2 large cans peas (drained)
⅓ cup / 100 ml. water
1 tsp. salt
1 tsp. pepper
1 tsp. sugar
3 shallots (minced)
2 tbsp. dill (chopped)
6 slices white bread (crusts removed)
⅔ cup / 150 ml. milk
3 eggs (beaten)
2 tbsp. butter

Place the peas in a saucepan with water, salt, pepper, sugar, shallots, and half the dill. Simmer 10 minutes. Moisten the bread in milk, then dip in eggs and fry in butter on both sides until golden brown. Drain the peas and pour over the fried bread. Sprinkle with the remaining dill.

# CHICKEN-LIVER PATE
## (paté de ficat de pasăre)

1 lb. / 500 g. chicken livers
½ lb. / 250 g. lard or margarine
4 onions (chopped)
1 tbsp. vegetable oil
⅓ cup / 100 g. flour
4 eggs (beaten)
3 tbsp. Armagnac or prune brandy
4 tbsp. port or sherry
1 tsp. paprika
1 tsp. garlic powder
Salt
Pepper

Cut the livers and lard into small pieces. Fry the onions until golden in the oil. In a bowl, mix the livers, lard, onions, flour, eggs, Armagnac, port, and seasonings. Spoon the mixture into a greased terrine dish and smooth the top. Cover with aluminum foil, place in a roasting pan containing 2 inches (5 cm.) of water, and bake at 325 degrees (170 degrees C) for about 1½ hours. Allow to cool and refrigerate until ready to serve.

# MARINATED OLIVES
## (măsline marinate)

---

2 lb. / 1 kg. black Greek olives
1 lemon
3 bay leaves
¾ cup / 200 ml. white-wine vinegar
1 tbsp. olive oil

Using a sharp knife, score the olives lengthwise. Place them in a large saucepan, cover with water, and bring to the boil. Drain off the water, cover with fresh water, and bring to the boil again. Drain the olives and allow to cool. Meanwhile, cut the lemon into thin slices. When the olives are cold, place in a large jar alternating layers of olives, bay leaves, and lemon slices. Bring the vinegar to the boil, allow to cool, and pour over the olives. Cover with a thin layer of olive oil. Seal the jar and allow to marinate 3 days.

# TOAST WITH ROQUEFORT BUTTER
# OR BLACK BUTTER
## (pîine cu unt de roqfort sau unt negru)

---

**ROQUEFORT BUTTER**
1 cup / 250 g. butter or margarine
2 oz. / 50 g. Roquefort cheese

**BLACK BUTTER**
1 cup / 250 g. butter or margarine
½ lb. / 250 g. pitted black olives

In a food processor, blend the butter and cheese or olives until the mixture becomes creamy and smooth. Keep refrigerated until needed. Serve on toasted baguette slices alternating black and white butters. Sprinkle with minced chives, if desired.

# WHEY CHEESE WITH DILL
## (urdă cu mărar)

These last three recipes go well with crackers. This cheese is a very common variety in Romania. The closest thing in flavor found elsewhere is ricotta cheese, although urdă has a firmer texture.

> 8 oz. / 250 g. urdă or ricotta cheese
> 2 oz. / 50 g. butter
> 1 tbsp. minced dill
> Salt

Blend the cheese and butter until it forms a paste. Mix in the dill and salt to taste. Can be served with sliced green onions or chives.


# TIMISHOARA-STYLE SPREAD
## (liptauer timişorean)

Timishoara is a city in the Banat region of Romania, very close to the borders with Hungary and Serbia. It is a prosperous city, now best known for being the heart of the 1989 revolution. In this recipe the paprika reflects a Hungarian influence.

> 8 oz. / 250 g. feta cheese
> ⅓ cup / 100 g. butter
> 1 tbsp. sweet paprika
> 1 tsp. finely ground caraway seeds
> Salt

Blend the cheese and butter until creamy. Add the paprika, caraway, and salt to taste and mix well. Serve with slices of radish on whole-wheat crackers, if desired.

# HERRING AND NUT SPREAD
## (pastă de hering cu nuci)

**Crusts of 2 slices bread**
**4 tbsp. milk + few drops vinegar**
**1 herring**
**3 tbsp. olive oil**
**½ onion (diced)**
**2 tsp. vinegar**
**12 ground walnuts**

Soak the bread crusts in milk containing a few drops of vinegar. Meanwhile, wash the herring and remove its skin and all the bones. (You may want to use a fillet prepared by your fishmonger.) Put the fish into a food processor along with the drained crusts and 1 tbsp. oil. Process, adding 1 tbsp. of oil at a time. Next add the onion, vinegar, and nuts and mix well. This can be served as a dip, spread on crackers, or on a fish-shaped dish with the real head and tail at either end for decoration.

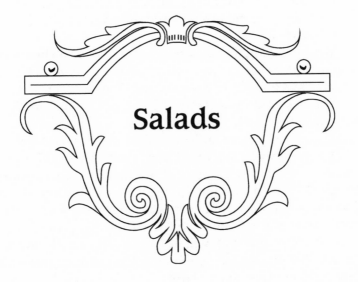

# Salads

When I was a little girl, my grandparents always sprinkled salt on vegetables, but I would kick up a fuss when they reached my plate. Every time this happened they would remind me of the story of the king and his three daughters. This fairy tale tells of an old king who one day decides that the time has come to divide his wealth amongst his daughters. In order to decide how much to give each one, he calls his daughters to him and asks them to tell him how they love him.

The eldest daughter answers, "Father, I love you like honey." The middle daughter answers, "Father, I love you like sweet wine." The youngest of the princesses then answers, "Father, I love you like salt in my food." The king is so appalled by this response that he shouts at his youngest child that he never wants to see her again and she should leave immediately.

The girl leaves the room and sadly walks through the palace to the kitchen, a place of respite where she spent most of her childhood running around and tasting from the pots. She seeks comfort from her friend, the elderly woman who is their cook. She tells the cook what has happened, and the cook decides that she will help the girl, as she loves her dearly. She plans to serve the king food with no salt for several days in order to convince him how wrong he is. As the days go by, the king gets more and more angry at the appalling food, cannot eat any of it, and begins to lose weight and become sad. Then one day the cook returns to cooking with salt. The young princess brings her father the meal. He at first refuses to eat from it, but succumbs in the end because he is so hungry. As he enjoys the food, his daughter explains that before there was no salt in the food and that is why it was so awful. She says, "Father, do you now see the importance of salt?"

The king finally realizes his mistake, embraces his daughter, and asks her for forgiveness. To show her how much he now appreciates her initial sentiment, he decides to give her the largest part of his kingdom.

These salads are quite simple to prepare and are traditionally presented on the table as starters, several of them together. They are a great favorite during hot Romanian summer lunches, eaten with thick slices of crusty country bread. And yes, most of them are flavored with salt.

# GRILLED PEPPER SALAD
## (salată de ardei copți)

This is a family favorite, still made by my mother and father for weekend lunches. It adds real flavor to a meal.

**12 large red or green bell peppers**
**3 tbsp. oil**
**1 tbsp. white-wine vinegar**
**3 cloves garlic (sliced)**
**Salt**

Grill the peppers evenly on all sides until the skin starts to bubble and darken, then lay them on a chopping board or plate and cover with plastic wrap. Leave for 20 minutes. Remove the wrap and gently clean the skins off the peppers, being careful to leave the flesh intact. Cut the tops off, remove all the seeds, and arrange the peppers in a casserole dish. Sprinkle over the oil, vinegar, garlic, and salt. Refrigerate at least 2 hours for the flavors to seep into the peppers. The peppers can be prepared days in advance.

# FRIED PEPPER SALAD
## (salată de ardei prăjiţi)

12 red and green bell peppers
5 small onions
3 tbsp. olive oil
1 cup / 250 ml. tomato purée
1 tbsp. sugar
Pinch salt

Cut the peppers into thin strips and dice the onions. Fry the onions in oil until they soften. Then add the peppers, purée, sugar, and salt. Simmer until the sauce reduces and allow to cool. Serve cold.

# AUBERGINE SALAD
## (salată de vinete)

This salad is a staple of Romanian cooking—if you haven't ever made it, or even tasted it, you cannot call yourself a Romanian. Good aubergine salad is creamy and pale in color. It is always served with onion, which I hated as a child. I would have to concentrate very hard while the salad was being served, to make sure that when some was served to me no onion would touch the plate. Otherwise I would annoy parents and grandparents by spending an hour picking onion out of my salad.

2 large aubergines (eggplants)
4 tbsp. olive oil
Salt
Pepper
1 small onion (diced)
2 tbsp. chopped parsley

Wrap the aubergines individually in aluminum foil and bake at 400 degrees (200 degrees C) until they feel soft to the touch inside the foil. This will take 30-45 minutes. Allow to cool slightly and remove the skins. Place the baked aubergines in a food processor with oil. Add salt and pepper to taste and blend until light and creamy. Pour onto a serving plate and decorate with the onion and parsley.

## FRIED AUBERGINE SALAD
### (salată de vinete prăjite)

2 large aubergines (eggplants)
5 tbsp. olive oil
5 medium onions (chopped)
5 green bell peppers (grilled and sliced into
    strips)
1 cup / 250 ml. tomato purée
Pinch salt
6 large lettuce leaves

Wrap the aubergines individually in aluminum foil and bake at 400 degrees (200 degrees C) until they feel soft to the touch inside the foil, 30 to 45 minutes. Allow to cool slightly and remove the skins. Chop the aubergines coarsely. In a hot pan containing the oil, cook the onions over low heat for 10 minutes until soft, then add the aubergines, peppers, purée, and salt. Simmer over medium heat about 10 minutes, stirring regularly, until the sauce reduces. Allow to cool completely and serve in lettuce leaves surrounded by a green salad, if desired.

# COURGETTE SALAD
## (salată de dovlecei)

3 courgettes (zucchini)
3 tbsp. olive oil
1 large onion (minced)
2 tsp. white-wine vinegar
Salt
Pepper
Tomatoes
Chopped dill

Cut the courgettes into large chunks, cover with salted water, and boil for 15 minutes until they soften. Drain and place the courgettes in a food processor with the oil. Mix until creamy. Add the onion, vinegar, and salt and pepper to taste. Serve over thinly sliced tomatoes and sprinkle with dill.

# POTATO SALAD
## (salată de cartofi)

1 lb. / 500 g. potatoes
2 large onions (sliced into rings)
Salt
1 large pickle (sliced)
3 tbsp. olive oil
1 tsp. vinegar
1 hard-boiled egg (sliced)

Boil the potatoes whole for 30-40 minutes, remove their skins, and allow to cool. Cut into thin slices and mix with the onions, salt, pickle, oil, and vinegar. Serve in a bowl of mixed salad leaves, decorated with slices of egg.

# RUSSIAN SALAD
## (salată rusească)

3 carrots (boiled)
3 potatoes (boiled with skins on)
½ lb. / 250 g. green beans (boiled)
½ lb. / 250 g. peas (boiled)
3 eggs (hard-boiled)
1 tsp. mustard
2 tbsp. mayonnaise
Salt
Pepper

Slice the carrots and potatoes, and cut the green beans in half. Place them together in a bowl, along with the peas. Remove the yolks from the hard-boiled eggs and discard the yolks. Dice the egg whites and add to the salad. Mix the vegetables, mustard, and mayonnaise, then add salt and pepper to taste.

# LEEK AND BEAN SALAD
## (salată de praz şi fasole)

1 lb. / 500 g. pinto beans (canned)
3 large leeks
3 tbsp. olive oil
2 cloves garlic (crushed)
2 tbsp. vinegar
Salt
1 tbsp. chopped dill

Rinse the beans and place in a large bowl. Cut the leeks into thin rings and add to the beans. Heat the olive oil in a frying pan, add the garlic, and, before it has time to brown, add the beans and leeks. Stir to coat the vegetables in the oil. Add the vinegar and salt and fry another 2 minutes. Allow the salad to cool, transfer to a serving dish, and sprinkle with dill.

## RED AND WHITE CABBAGE SALAD
### (salată de varză rosie şi albă)

1 medium red cabbage
1 medium white cabbage
Salt
4 tbsp. olive oil
5-6 tbsp. white-wine vinegar
½ tbsp. sugar

Wash the cabbage and cut into very thin strips. Add a few teaspoons of salt and rub it into the cabbage with your hands until the cabbage softens. Using a tea towel squeeze the liquid out of the cabbage. Transfer the cabbage to a bowl, add the oil, vinegar, and sugar, and mix well.

## RADISH SALAD
### (salată de ridichi)

3 bunches radishes
1 egg (hard-boiled)
3 tbsp. sour cream
Salt

Cut the radishes into thin slices and transfer to a bowl. Crush the hard-boiled egg yolk and beat together with the sour cream. Pour the sour cream mixture over the radishes. Cut the egg white into a fine dice and add to the bowl. Add salt. Mix well.

# VEGETABLE AND APPLE SALAD
### (salată din crudități cu mere)

1 lb. / 250 g. apples
2 tbsp. lemon juice
5 oz. / 150 g. celery (thinly sliced)
4 oz. / 100 g. carrots (thinly sliced)
Salt
⅓ cup / 100 ml. sour cream
4 oz. / 100 g. lettuce leaves

Peel the apples. Cut one apple into thin slices and the rest into fine strips. Cover with the lemon juice. Mix together the apple strips, celery, carrots, salt, and sour cream. Serve in cups lined with lettuce leaves and covered with sliced apple.


# HERRING AND ONION SALAD
### (salată de scrumbii cu ceapă)

3 herrings
3 small red onions
4 oz. / 100 g. black olives (pitted)
3 tbsp. olive oil
2 tbsp. vinegar

Clean out the herrings and rinse in plenty of water. Remove the skins by pulling from head to tail. Remove the spine and large bones. Cut the herrings into 1-inch (3-cm.) slices and arrange on a plate. Cut the onions into thin rings and arrange over the fish. Next cover with the olives, and drizzle the oil and vinegar over all.

# FISH ROE SALAD
## (salată de icre)

---

9 oz. / 300 g. carp or pike roe
2 tbsp. breadcrumbs (soaked in 1 tbsp. milk)
½ cup / 125 ml. vegetable oil
Juice of 1 lemon
1 onion (diced)
Black olives

Place the roe in a bowl and add the breadcrumbs. Mix with a wooden spoon, adding the oil in a fine stream while continuing to mix. Then add the lemon juice and homogenize the mixture again. This should form a paste the same texture as mayonnaise. Serve with the onions on the side, decorated with black olives.

# CHICKEN SALAD
## (salată de pasăre)

---

5 chicken drumsticks
3 cups / 750 ml. chicken stock
3 apples
4 celery stalks
2 tbsp. lemon juice
2 potatoes (boiled and cubed)
⅔ cup / 150 ml. mayonnaise
1 tbsp. mustard
Salt
Pepper

Boil the drumsticks in chicken stock for 45 minutes, until the meat is cooked and easily comes off the bone. Discard the bones and skin, then pull the meat apart into shreds. Dice the apples and celery, then place them in a bowl containing cold water and the lemon juice. This will keep the apples from browning. In another bowl, mix the potatoes, celery, apples, mayonnaise, and mustard. Finally add the chicken, and salt and pepper to taste.

# SALAD A LA PRAGUE
## (salată à la praga)

Anyone who has ever smelled the leaves of a tomato plant will know how distinctive they smell. This is one of the smells that evokes my childhood. I spent so many hours hiding from my brothers in the vegetable garden that tomatoes are for me the smell of hide-and-seek. A vegetable garden is wonderful to watch in any season. In spring, the pointy tips of the onions would start showing in neat rows. In summer there were always the beautiful yellow flowers that would amazingly produce courgettes. I would stare at the majestic sunflowers, wondering when the time would come when I could eat the seeds. Other fragrances come to mind, like thyme—and colors, celery and white aubergine flowers.

One of the most fun errands I would be sent on was to gather fresh tomatoes, cucumbers, and onions in a wicker basket for my grandmother. Then I would watch her prepare a wonderful salad, which we would eat with freshly baked brown bread.

> ½ lb. / 250 g. salami
> 4 oz. / 100 g. peas (canned)
> 5 oz. / 150 g. carrots (boiled and sliced)
> 5 oz. / 150 g. pickles (chopped)
> 1 tsp. mustard
> 1 large red bell pepper (diced)
> 2 tbsp. mayonnaise
> 1 tsp. salt
> ½ tsp. pepper
> 1 tbsp. chopped parsley
> 2 large tomatoes

Cut the salami into small cubes. Mix with the drained peas, carrots, pickles, mustard, red pepper, and mayonnaise. Add salt and pepper, mix well, and serve sprinkled with parsley on a bed of thin tomato slices.

# TONGUE SALAD
## (salată cu limbă de vită)

1 lb. / 500 g. beef or veal tongue
Beef stock to cover
2 tsp. salt
1 bay leaf
1 tsp. paprika
2 onions (sliced)
4 tomatoes (sliced)
3 large red bell peppers (sliced)
3 eggs (hard-boiled)
Juice of 1 lemon
½ tsp. salt
½ tsp. pepper
2 tbsp. chopped parsley

Boil the tongue in beef stock with 2 tsp. salt, bay leaf, and paprika. Once the tongue has cooked and cooled, cut half the tongue in thin slices and the other in fine strips. Then mix the strips with the onions, tomatoes, and peppers. Place the mixture in a peaked mound in the center of a dish. Cover the mound with the remaining tongue slices, layering one slice slightly over the last one, going all the way around. Next decorate with the sliced eggs.

Make the dressing by mixing together the lemon juice, ½ tsp. salt, the pepper, and parsley. Pour over the salad.

# Soups

Romanian winters can get very cold and snowy, especially in the north of the country. My mother was born at home on a morning in early January. According to my mother's aunt, the snow was at least 5 feet high and she was sent to her sister's house with baskets of supplies. She was a teenager at the time and had to carefully make her way in the dark, on slippery paths made through huge mounds of snow, carrying the heavy parcels.

The need for warmth and sustenance during these cold winters is the reason for the enormous number of soup variations in Romania. These are a few of the classic recipes, as well as some that my grandmother found more interesting.

# VEGETABLE SOUP WITH SOUR CREAM
## (supă de zarzavat cu smintîna)

¾ gal. / 3 l. water
1 large onion (cut into strips)
1 carrot (cut into strips)
1 large bunch parsley
1 can cut green beans
2 potatoes (peeled and cubed)
4 tomatoes (peeled, seeded, and diced)
Pinch salt
1 tbsp. butter or margarine
1 tbsp. flour
⅔ cup / 150 ml. sour cream
Chopped fresh dill and parsley

In a large pot, bring the water to the boil with the onion, carrot, parsley, green beans, and potatoes. Allow to simmer on medium heat 20 minutes, then add the tomatoes and salt. Mix together the butter and flour to form a paste, then add to the soup, mixing slowly until the soup thickens. Cover and simmer a few more minutes. Serve in bowls topped with a spoonful of sour cream and sprinkled with dill and parsley.

# CAULIFLOWER SOUP
## (supă de conopidă)

---

½ gal. / 2 l. water
1 carrot (grated)
1 large bunch parsley (chopped)
1 large onion (grated)
1 tbsp. butter
1 tbsp. flour
Salt
Pepper
1 medium cauliflower (cut in small florets)
⅔ cup / 150 ml. sour cream
1 tbsp. chopped dill

Bring the water to the boil with the carrot, parsley, and onion. Simmer over medium heat for 20 minutes until they soften. Mix the butter and flour together to form a paste, dilute in a spoonful of the soup, and add this to the pot with some salt and pepper. Add the cauliflower florets and simmer about 30 minutes, until the cauliflower is soft. Mix the sour cream with the dill and add to the soup.

# CREAMY POTATO SOUP
## (supă de cartofi)

---

½ gal. / 2 l. water
1 lb. / 500 g. potatoes (cubed)
1 onion (chopped)
1 clove garlic (crushed)
1 tsp. salt
1 cup / 250 ml. sour cream
1 tbsp. flour
1 tbsp. chopped parsley
1 tbsp. butter

In the water, boil the potatoes, onion, and garlic until soft, about 20 minutes. Using a hand-held liquidizer or a blender, liquidize the potatoes and water. Add salt and bring to the boil again. When the soup starts to boil, add the sour cream mixed with the flour. Simmer on medium for 20 minutes, then add the parsley and butter. Serve with toasted bread.

# TOMATO SOUP
## (supă de roşii)

---

2 lb. / 1 kg. tomatoes
6 cups / 1½ l. water
1 large carrot (grated)
1 large bunch parsley
1 onion (grated)
2 tbsp. white rice
2 large green bell peppers (quartered)
Salt
1 tbsp. sugar
2 tbsp. oil
1 tbsp. flour
Chopped parsley
Chopped celery leaves
1 tbsp. chopped dill

Cut the tomatoes into quarters and boil in 2 cups (½ l.) water for about 30 minutes. When the tomatoes have softened, drain them. In a clean pot, in 4 cups (1 l.) water, add the carrot, parsley, and onion. Simmer over medium heat until all the vegetables have softened, about 20 minutes. Drain the vegetables, reserving the cooking liquid in the pot. Now add the tomatoes, rice, peppers, salt, and sugar to the liquid. Bring to the boil and simmer on low heat, covered, until the rice is half-cooked, about 10 minutes.

In a small pan, cook the oil and flour until well mixed, then add to the soup. Continue to simmer until the rice is completely cooked. Then add the chopped parsley, celery leaves, and dill. This soup is delicious cold as well as hot.

# CREAM OF SPINACH SOUP
## (supă de spanac)

1 lb. / 500 g. fresh spinach
¾ gal. / 3 l. water
1 slice lemon
1 tbsp. chopped chives
1 tsp. salt
1 tbsp. butter
1 tsp. flour
⅓ cup / 100 ml. sour cream

Wash the spinach and place in a pot with the water. Bring to the boil and simmer on medium heat for 20 minutes. Remove from the heat and, using a hand-held liquidizer or a blender, liquidize the spinach and water. Reheat, adding the lemon, chives, salt, and butter. Allow to simmer on medium heat another 30 minutes. Then mix the flour with the sour cream and add to the soup. Serve with savory pancakes, if desired.

# CREAM OF CARROT SOUP
## (supă de morcovi)

1 lb. / 500 g. carrots (cut into strips)
1 large onion (cut into strips)
1 clove garlic (crushed)
¾ gal. / 3 l. water
½ tbsp. sugar
1 tsp. salt
1 tbsp. butter
⅓ cup / 100 ml. sour cream
Croutons

Place the carrots, onion, garlic and water in a large pot and bring to the boil. Allow to simmer on medium heat until the vegetables soften, about 20 minutes. Using a hand-held liquidizer or a blender, liquidize the soup and reheat, this time adding the sugar, salt, and butter. Simmer on medium heat another 10 minutes. Drizzle sour cream over each bowl and top with several croutons.

## BUTTER-BEAN CREAM SOUP
### (supă de fasole boabe)

¾ gal. / 3 l. water
8 oz. / 250 g. butter beans (canned)
1 large onion (chopped)
1 carrot
1 bunch fresh parsley
1 tbsp. butter or oil
1 tsp. salt
Chopped fresh parsley
½ tsp. pepper
Croutons

In a large pot with the water, add the beans, onion, whole carrot, and whole parsley. Bring to the boil and simmer on medium heat for 40 minutes, covered. Remove the carrot and parsley and, using a hand-held liquidizer or a blender, liquidize the bean soup. Add the butter and salt and simmer for another 15 minutes. Then add the chopped parsley and pepper. Serve with croutons.

# GREEN CORN SOUP
## (supă de porumb verde)

If anyone would ask me what reminds me the most of my grandmother, it would have to be soups. Any soup, and the smell of dill that was often associated with it, reminds me of her, because she could make so many different ones. It was always so comforting in the winters. My brothers and I were picky eaters, but Grandma's soups were always a hit. Big steamy bowls of hearty soup and a good piece of cornbread would be waiting for us after school. This would give us the necessary fuel for an afternoon of games and study.

1½ gal. / 6 l. water
1 lb. / 500 g. corn (canned)
1 bunch fresh parsley
1 carrot (chopped)
1 large onion (chopped)
1 tbsp. flour
1½ cups / 400 ml. milk
1 tbsp. butter
2 tsp. salt
1 egg (hard-boiled and diced)
½ tbsp. chopped dill

In a large pot with the water, add the corn, parsley, carrot, and onion and bring to the boil. Simmer on medium heat for 30 minutes. Using a hand-held liquidizer or a blender, liquidize the soup and reheat. Mix together the flour, milk, butter, and salt. Add to the soup. Simmer for another 15 minutes. Serve with diced egg and dill sprinkled over the soup.

# LENTIL SOUP
## (supă de linte)

½ lb. / 250 g. lentils
¾ gal / 3 l. water
1 large onion (chopped)
2 cloves garlic
1 tsp. salt
1 tbsp. flour
2 tbsp. oil
½ tbsp. chopped fresh thyme

Soak the lentils in warm water overnight, then rinse them well. In a large pot, in the cold water, add the lentils, onion, and garlic cloves. Bring to the boil and simmer on medium heat until the lentils start to soften, about 20 minutes. Then add the salt and continue to simmer until the lentils are thoroughly cooked, another 20 minutes. In a small bowl, mix together the flour, oil, and thyme with 1 tbsp. soup. Mix into the pot, simmer another 15 minutes, and serve.

# CUMIN SOUP
## (supă cu chimen)

10 cups / 2½ l. fish stock
⅓ cup / 100 g. flour
1-2 tbsp. cold water
2 tbsp. cumin
1 tsp. paprika
Salt

Bring the stock to the boil. Dissolve the flour in the water, then add to the stock. Simmer 15 minutes on medium heat. Next add the cumin, paprika, and salt, and simmer another 5 minutes. Serve with noodles or croutons.

# GARLIC SOUP
## (supă de usturoi)

10 cups / 2½ l. vegetable stock
6 cloves garlic (minced)
1 tsp. minced thyme
½ tsp. cloves
Salt
Pepper
3 slices bread
5 oz. / 150 g. shredded mozzarella or cheddar
   cheese
2 tbsp. olive oil

Bring the stock to the boil with the garlic, thyme, cloves, salt, and pepper. Simmer on medium heat for 20 minutes. Strain the resulting soup and discard the solids. Cut each slice of bread into quarters and place on a cookie sheet. Cover with the cheese and drizzle with olive oil. Place under the broiler until the cheese has melted (about 5 minutes). When ready serve 2 pieces of bread in every bowl of soup.

# BEEF SOUP
## (supă de carne de vacă)

2 lb. / 1 kg. beef (cubed)
¾ gal. / 3 l. water
2 carrots (chopped)
10 celery stalks (chopped)
1 large green bell pepper (chopped)
1 large onion (chopped)
5 peppercorns
1 bay leaf
1 bunch fresh parsley
½ tsp. salt

Bring the meat to the boil in the water and simmer uncovered on medium heat until foam rises, about 15 minutes. Remove the foam and simmer beef another 30 minutes, removing the foam continuously until it stops forming. Add the vegetables, peppercorns, bay leaf, parsley, and salt. Cover the pot, leaving a small opening, and simmer on low heat for 3 hours. Serve with Romanian Soup Noodles (see end of chapter) or rice.

## TRADITIONAL BORSCHT
### (borş)

Borscht is an Eastern European dish that is recognized around the world. Anyone who has experienced the harsh winters of Russia, Poland, Romania, etc., knows why this hearty soup is so popular. There are many variations; the ones here have been made in my family for years.

> 2 lb. / 1 kg. beef (in large cubes)
> ⅔ gal. / 2½ l. water
> 1 tbsp. tomato paste
> ½ cabbage (in strips)
> 2 carrots (grated)
> 2 carrots (whole)
> 3 potatoes (diced)
> 1 green bell pepper (whole)
> 2 red beets (grated)
> 2 red beets (whole)
> Juice of 1 lemon
> Salt
> Pepper
> Crème fraîche

In a large pot, bring the beef to the boil in the water. Remove any foam that forms. Add the tomato paste and all the vegetables except the 2 whole beets. Bring to the boil, then reduce the heat to low. Leave to simmer 1½ hours. Now add the beets to reinforce the color, as well as the lemon juice, salt, and pepper, and allow to simmer another 15 minutes. When the meat is cooked through, remove it from the soup. Also remove the whole vegetables. Only the liquid and cut vegetables are eaten in the soup. Serve each bowl with a spoonful of crème fraîche. The meat can be eaten cold accompanied by a green salad and roasted potatoes.

## GREEN BEAN BORSCHT
### (borş de fasole verde)

8 cups / 2 l. salted water
1 small carrot (chopped)
1 small bunch parsley (not chopped)
1 onion (diced)
¾ lb. / 300 g. cut green beans
1 green bell pepper (sliced)
4 tomatoes (peeled and sliced)
1 tbsp. olive oil
½ tbsp. flour
2 cups / ½ l. Traditional Borscht (see recipe above)

Bring the water, carrot, parsley, and onion to the boil. Add the green beans and, after boiling for several minutes, add the pepper and tomatoes. In a small pan, heat the oil over high heat and cook the flour in it for about 1 minute, stirring. Add 1 tbsp. liquid from the soup, mix well, then add the mixture to the soup. Simmer on medium heat until the beans are soft, about 15 minutes. Now add the borscht and simmer another 10 minutes. Serve hot or cold.

# VEAL BORSCHT
## (borş de viţel)

8 cups / 2 l. water
1½ lb. / 750 g. veal (cubed)
1 tsp. salt
1 onion (quartered)
5 stalks celery (in large pieces)
1 carrot (cut into four pieces)
1 bunch parsley (coarsely torn)
1 tbsp. white rice
4 cups / 1 l. Traditional Borscht (see recipe)
Chopped celery leaves
1 egg

Boil the water and veal, removing any foam that forms until the liquid becomes clear. This should take 20-30 minutes. Add salt, onion, celery, carrot, and parsley. Cover and simmer on medium-low heat until the meat is cooked through, about 30 minutes. Now add the rice and borscht and simmer for 20 minutes, until the rice is cooked. Add the celery leaves. Just before serving the hot soup, beat the egg and add to the soup, mixing continuously.

# UKRANIAN BORSCHT
## (borş ucrainean)

This is a slightly different version of the veal borscht, this time with more beet and tomato added in. Follow the recipe above, but add 2 chopped red beets and 2 large chopped tomatoes when adding the other vegetables.

# MOLDAVIAN BORSCHT
## (borş moldovenesc)

This recipe is from the northeastern region of Romania. Follow the Veal Borscht recipe, but after the rice has cooked, add 3 tbsp. chopped celeriac, 2 tbsp. chopped celery leaves, and 3 or 4 large pickles, cut into big chunks.

# BORSCHT WITH FISH BALLS
## (borş cu perişoare de peşte)

8 cups / 2 l. water
2 onions (sliced)
1 carrot (sliced)
1 bunch parsley (not chopped)
1 lb. / 500 g. carp (whole)
1 thick slice white bread soaked in milk (crust removed)
1 tbsp. chopped dill
1 tbsp. chopped parsley
Salt
Pepper
1 egg
4 cups / 1 l. Traditional Borscht (see recipe)

In a pot with the water, place 1 onion, the carrot, and the parsley. Add the head and tail of the carp and simmer on medium heat 30 minutes. Meanwhile, fillet the fish and remove its skin. Then chop up the fish in a food processor with the remaining onion, the bread, herbs, salt, pepper, and egg. Shape the mixture into small balls. Now separate the soup liquid from the vegetables and fish. Remove the fish head and tail from the vegetables. In a clean pot, reheat the soup liquid and vegetables, this time adding the fish balls and borscht. Simmer 20 minutes and serve.

# RUSSIAN CHORBA
## (ciorbă rusească)

*Ciorbă* is *the* Romanian soup. It differs from other soups in that it is heartier, like borscht, and often contains cabbage and meat, giving it a sweet and sour taste. Here are a few versions.

**1 lb. / 500 g. beef (in cubes)**
**¾ gal. / 3 l. water**
**1 tsp. salt**
**1 red beet (shredded)**
**1 onion (shredded)**
**1 carrot (shredded)**
**Chopped dill**
**1 large green bell pepper (cut into strips)**
**10 large string beans (cut into squares)**
**½ white cabbage (diced)**
**1 lb. / 500 g. tomatoes (peeled and diced)**
**2 tbsp. chopped parsley**

Boil the beef in the water on medium heat. Keep removing foam that forms until the broth is clear. Add salt and simmer until the meat is cooked, about 30 minutes. Add the beet, onion, carrot, and dill and continue to simmer another 30-45 minutes. Next add the pepper, beans, and cabbage and simmer another 15 minutes. Lastly add the tomatoes, bring to the boil once, then add the parsley and serve.

# LAMB CHORBA
## (ciorbă de miel)

2 lb. / 1 kg. shoulder of lamb (cubed)
8 cups / 2 l. water
1 lb. / 500 g. fresh spinach
1 carrot (grated)
2 celery stalks (chopped)
1 onion (chopped)
1 clove garlic (crushed)
Salt
Pepper
3 tbsp. white rice
1 egg yolk

In a large pot, bring the meat to the boil in the water, removing any foam that forms, then simmer for 30 minutes. Cut the spinach coarsely. Add it, the remaining vegetables, the garlic, salt, and pepper to the soup. Continue to simmer 20 minutes. Add the rice and simmer another 20 minutes. Beat the egg yolk and pour into the soup, mixing all the time. Serve immediately.

# CABBAGE AND SMOKED-MEAT CHORBA
## (ciorbă de varză cu afumătură)

¾ lb. / 400 g. smoked chicken breast
1 lb. / 500 g. white cabbage (sliced)
2 cloves garlic (crushed)
¾ gal. / 3 l. chicken stock
¾ lb. / 400 g. potatoes (sliced)
5 oz. / 150 g. button mushrooms
Salt
Pepper
2 tbsp. chopped parsley

Cut the chicken into cubes. Add the chicken, cabbage, and

garlic to a pot of hot stock. Bring to the boil, then simmer 20 minutes. Now add the potatoes and mushrooms, as well as some salt and pepper. Continue to simmer another ½ hour or until the potatoes soften. Add the chopped parsley just before serving.

## PEASANT CHICKEN CHORBA
### (ciorbă ţărănească cu carne de pui)

1 lb. / 500 g. chicken meat (cut into strips)
6 cups / 1½ l. water
Salt
4 carrots (chopped)
4 oz. / 100 g. celeriac (chopped)
2 onions (chopped)
1 red bell pepper (cut in strips)
4 oz. / 100 g. parsnips (chopped)
½ lb. / 250 g. potatoes (cubed)
4 oz. / 100 g. white cabbage (cut in strips)
2 tbsp. tomato paste diluted in 2 tbsp. water
4 oz. / 100 g. butter beans (canned)
½ lb. / 250 g. tomatoes (sliced)
2 tbsp. chopped celery leaves
2 tbsp. chopped parsley
4 cups / 1 l. Traditional Borscht (see recipe)
1 tsp. salt
2 tbsp. chopped dill

Bring the meat to the boil in the water with some salt. Remove any foam that forms while simmering for 20 minutes. Now add the carrots, celeriac, onions, pepper, parsnips, potatoes, and cabbage. Simmer another ½ hour. Then add the tomato paste. Add the beans, tomatoes, celery leaves, parlsey, borscht, and 1 tsp. salt and simmer for a final 20 minutes. Serve very hot with dill sprinkled on top.

# ROMANIAN SOUP NOODLES
## (zdrenţe si taiţei)

**ZDRENŢE**
**2 eggs**
**3 tbsp. flour**
**Pinch salt**

In a bowl, beat the eggs, then add the flour bit by bit, along with salt. Beat the mixture to form a thick batter. While your soup is boiling, pour the batter very slowly into the soup, in a thin stream, with the help of a fork. Then allow the soup to simmer 15 minutes. Thin filaments of noodles will form as the batter cooks in the soup.

**TAIŢEI**
**1 cup / 250 g. flour**
**3 eggs**
**½ tsp. salt**
**2 tbsp. water**

On a wooden board, pour the flour into a mound and make a hole in the center. Break the eggs in the well and mix with a bit of the flour. Add the salt and water bit by bit and mix into a dough, adding more flour if necessary. Divide the dough into 3 pieces and knead each piece. Shape into balls and cover. Leave for 10 minutes.

On a floured surface, roll out each piece into a sheet as thin as possible. Place the sheets on a clean floured towel and leave to dry. When the sheets are half-dried, cut them into strips 1¼ inch wide (3 cm.), then pile up 4-5 strips and cut into very thin pieces. Leave to dry completely on a plate, about 15-20 minutes. Add to boiling soups and simmer 10 minutes.

# Fish

The variety of fish available in Romania is significant thanks to the presence of the Danube Delta, the point where the Danube River spills into the Black Sea after its journey of some 1,700 miles from the springs of Donaueschingen in Germany. The Danube River and its delta are an ecological treasure, with over 200 species of bird and 90 species of fish. The fish varieties such as perch, carp, mackerel, and sturgeon are all used in Romanian recipes, some of which you will find below.

When I was growing up, fish was very common at my grandmother's table. It smelled wonderful and my brothers and I loved eating it, but we were taught always to allow the grownups to prepare it for us. Someone checked the pieces for small bones before any fish was even allowed on our plates. This turned eating fish into a very mature thing and I always aspired to being old enough to eat fish on my own. My older brother once got a tiny bone stuck in his throat when he was four years old and my grandmother never forgave herself for her carelessness.

Another childhood memory is of my other grandmother, also of Romanian origin, once preparing a fish and throwing the distended bladder on the floor, for me to step on and hear it pop. After that, I was always very disappointed when no bladder was produced for me to enjoy. I couldn't understand why smaller fish didn't have the same balloon.

# ROMANIAN FRIED CARP
## (plachie de crap)

If carp is not available, trout can be used as an alternative in the following recipes.

> 2 lb. / 1 kg. carp fillet
> Salt
> 2 tbsp. flour
> 4 tbsp. olive oil
> 5 large onions (sliced)
> 1 tbsp. vegetable or fish stock
> 1 cup / 250 ml. dry white wine
> 5 peppercorns
> Lemon slices

Cut the carp fillet into 2½-inch pieces (6 cm.). Sprinkle the slices with salt and leave for 15 minutes. Wipe the fish clean with paper towels and roll in flour. Heat up a frying pan containing the oil and fry the fish over medium heat, about 5 minutes on each side. Turn the pieces over carefully so as not to break them. When the fish is fried, remove onto a plate. In the remaining oil, cook the onions until they begin to brown. Now add the stock, wine, salt, peppercorns, and lemon slices. Simmer for 2-3 minutes, then transfer the mixture to an ovenproof dish, arranging the onions over the surface of the dish. Top with the fried carp and bake at 350 degrees (180 degrees C) for 20 minutes. This dish can be served hot with potatoes or rice, or cold in the summer, accompanied by a salad.

# CARP ON RICE
## (crap pe orez)

2 lb. / 1 kg. carp fillet
Salt
1 onion (chopped)
4 tbsp. olive oil
7 oz. / 200 g. white rice
Water
Pepper
1 tsp. flour
2 tbsp. white-wine vinegar
Chopped parsley
Lemon slices

Cut the carp into slices of 1½-inch slices (4 cm.) and sprinkle with salt. Leave the fish for 30 minutes. Meanwhile, cook the onion in the olive oil until it just starts browning. Wash the rice and add to the frying pan. Continue to cook until the rice starts to brown a little. Add as much water as necessary to cover the rice and leave to simmer for 5-6 minutes. Transfer the rice and onion to an ovenproof dish and sprinkle with salt and pepper. After patting the fish slices dry with paper towel, place them over the rice. To make the sauce, in a small bowl mix the flour and vinegar and pour over the fish. Bake at 350 degrees (180 degrees C) for about 30 minutes, adding water when necessary so that the rice doesn't dry out. Serve sprinkled with chopped parsley and slices of lemon.

# MARINATED CARP
## (marinată de crap)

2 lb. / 1 kg. carp fillet
Salt
2 tbsp. flour
3 tbsp. olive oil
1 tbsp. white-wine vinegar
½ cup / 125 ml. water
4 peppercorns
2 bay leaves
2 tsp. sugar
1 lemon (sliced)
Chopped fresh dill

Cut the fish into slices about 1¼ inches wide (3 cm.), sprinkle with salt on both sides, and leave for 30 minutes. Dry each slice of fish with paper towels. Then cover each slice with flour and fry in a pan containing the oil, over medium heat. Turn after 3 minutes and continue to fry until both sides are golden brown. Place the fish in a deep dish and set aside. To make the marinade, place the vinegar, water, peppercorns, bay leaves, sugar, and a pinch of salt in a saucepan. Bring to the boil and simmer on medium heat approximately 10 minutes. After allowing the marinade to cool, pour over the fish. Leave to marinate several hours or up to 2-3 days, after which it can be served hot or cold, garnished with slices of lemon and sprinkled with fresh dill.

# CARP GHIVECH
## (ghiveci cu crap)

Ghivech is a dish that consists of cooked or stewed vegetables. It is eaten hot or cold, alone or alongside meat or fish. In this recipe it is used to add flavor to the fish.

   2 large onions
   4 carrots
   3 tbsp. chopped celery leaves
   6 tbsp. vegetable oil
   5 tbsp. water
   1 lb. / 500 g. potatoes
   3 red bell peppers
   4 tbsp. tomato paste
   ¾ cup / 180 ml. boiling water
   ¼ lb. / 120 g. soaked peas
   ¼ lb. / 120 g. string beans
   4 large tomatoes (sliced)
   2 tbsp. chopped dill
   4 cloves garlic (sliced)
   2 sprigs thyme
   2 tsp. pepper
   3 tsp. salt
   2 lb. / 1 kg. carp fillet
   ½ cup / 125 ml. dry white wine

Cut the onions and carrots into strips. Add the celery leaves and cover with oil and the 5 tbsp. water. Meanwhile cut the potatoes into cubes and the peppers into strips. Add to the onions. In a cup mix the tomato paste with the boiling water and add to the vegetables. Now mix in the peas, beans, and tomatoes (reserve 6 slices). Spread the vegetables over the bottom of a baking pan and sprinkle with the dill, garlic, thyme, pepper, and salt.

Cut the fish into 6 equal pieces and lay over the vegetables. Place a slice of tomato onto each piece. Cover with the wine and bake at 350 degrees (180 degrees C) until the fish is cooked through, about 30 minutes.

## PICKLED CARP
### (saramură de crap)

2 lb. / 1 kg. carp fillet
Salt
3 cups / 750 ml. hot water
1 tsp. paprika
2 small chili peppers (seeded and sliced)
1 tsp. chopped dill
1 tbsp. vinegar

Clean the fish, cut into strips, sprinkle with salt, and lay in a baking pan. Make the cooking liquid by mixing the water with the paprika, peppers, dill, and vinegar. Pour over the fish and bake at 375 degrees (200 degrees C) until the liquid comes to the boil, about 10 minutes. Serve hot or cold.

## POLISH-STYLE PERCH
### (şalău polonez)

2 lb. / 1 kg. whole perch
1 large carrot
1 onion (coarsely chopped)
3 tbsp. coarsely chopped parsley
2-3 peppercorns
Water to cover
Juice of 1 lemon
3-4 large potatoes (in small cubes)
Butter or margarine
1 tbsp. flour
2 egg yolks
1 tbsp. sour cream
Salt

Wash the fish and cut off the fins with kitchen scissors. Next remove the scales (this should be done as soon as possible; otherwise it becomes a difficult task) and gut the fish through the gills by inserting a finger into the gill cavity and drawing out the entrails in one piece. Thoroughly rinse out the body cavity and leave the perch whole. Place in a large pot with the carrot, onion, 2 tbsp. parsley, and the peppercorns. Add enough water to cover. Simmer gently over medium heat until the fish is cooked (about 30 minutes or until the meat is firmer to the touch) and leave to cool in the pot. Now remove the fish and split it to clean out the spine, taking great care to preserve the fish's shape. Lay the fish on a long plate, drizzle the lemon juice over it, and cover to keep warm.

Remove the vegetables and peppercorns from the pot, reserving the stock, and boil the potatoes in the liquid. Meanwhile, in a small frying pan, melt a pat of butter, add the flour, then add a spoonful of fish stock and simmer over medium heat for about 2 minutes, mixing so that no lumps form. Mix the egg yolks into the sour cream and add to the pan. Mix well, then add this liquid and some salt to the potatoes after they have been cooked and drained. Mix well, pour the potatoes onto the fish, and sprinkle with remaining chopped parsley.

# POACHED MAYONNAISE PERCH
## (şalău cu maioneză)

2 lb. / 1 kg. perch
Salt
10 cups / 2½ l. fish stock
1 onion (chopped)
1 tsp. pepper
1 carrot (chopped)
1 bay leaf
2 potatoes (chopped)
2 tbsp. lemon juice
1 cup / 250 ml. mayonnaise
3 tbsp. chopped dill
6 sheets gelatin

Clean the fish, sprinkle with salt, and leave for 15 minutes. Meanwhile, in a fish poacher, bring the fish stock, onion, pepper, salt, carrot, and bay leaf to the boil. Simmer 15 minutes on medium heat. Add the potatoes and simmer another 15 minutes. Now place the fish on the poaching rack and lower into the liquid. Cover and simmer on low heat about 30 minutes, until the fish feels firm to the touch.

Allow the fish to cool slightly before removing from the poacher. Transfer onto a dish. Carefully cut the fish down the middle and remove the spine and bones, taking care not to flake the meat. Cut into large pieces, place on a serving plate, cover with lemon juice, and place a dollop of mayonnaise on each piece. Sprinkle with dill. Transfer the cooked vegetables to a shallow dish. Strain 6 cups (1½ l.) of the poaching liquid and transfer to a saucepan. Heat the liquid gently and dissolve the gelatin. Pour over the vegetables and refrigerate until set. Serve slices of the aspic with the poached fish.

# SKATE IN RED WINE
## (calcan în vin roşu)

This fish is not as common in Romania as carp or sturgeon but is interesting to cook. It is flat and has firm, white flesh. Its sweet taste is sometimes compared to that of scallops.

> 2 lb. / 1 kg. skate (ray) fillet
> Salt
> 1 carrot
> 1 onion
> Parsley
> 2 cloves
> 3 peppercorns
> 1 bay leaf
> ⅔ cup / 150 ml. dry red wine
> 4-5 tbsp. water
> 1 lb. / 500 g. small potatoes (whole)
> 1 tbsp. butter or margarine
> 1 tbsp. flour

Wash the fish well to get rid of the ammonia smell, then cut the fillet into 2x3-inch pieces (5x7 cm.). Salt the fish and leave for 30 minutes. Meanwhile slice the carrot and onion and place in a layer at the bottom of a deep pan, along with some parsley. Place the fish on top of the vegetables and add the cloves, peppercorns, and bay leaf. Add the wine and water. Place the pan on high heat and allow the liquid to come to the boil. At this stage, reduce to low heat, cover the pan, and simmer for about 15 minutes. The fish is ready when a toothpick easily slides into the thickest part of the fillet.

While the fish is cooking, boil the potatoes, then cut them into quarters. Once the fish is ready, carefully remove the liquid from the pan and transfer to a clean one. Mix the butter and flour, then add to the cooking liquid. Heat gently until the sauce begins to thicken, then remove from the heat. On a large serving plate, arrange the potatoes in the center with the pieces of fish around and the sauce covering the potatoes and fish.

## STUFFED BAKED PIKE
### (ştiucă umplute la cuptor)

2 lb. / 1 kg. whole pike (or perch)
Salt
3 large onions
3 tbsp. oil
1 large slice white bread soaked in milk (crust removed)
1 tsp. salt
1 tsp. pepper
1 tbsp. chopped parsley
2 eggs (beaten)
Lemon

Clean the pike of its fins and entrails, and cut off the head and tail, reserving the head. Starting at the head, peel the fish of its skin, keeping the skin intact. Salt the skin and put aside. Chop the onions, cook in some of the oil until golden brown, and place in a food processor. Take the fish meat off the bone and add to the onions, along with the bread. Add salt, pepper, parsley, and eggs. Mix everything until well blended. Now "stuff" the skin with the fish mixture, in the original shape of the fish, joining all the ends with toothpicks. Do not overstuff the skin or it will burst during cooking. If any mixture is left over, form small fish balls out of it. Place the stuffed fish, fish balls, and head in a long casserole dish, brush with remaining oil, and bake at 350 degrees (180 degrees C) for 30-40 minutes. Every so often, baste the fish with the oil from the bottom of the casserole dish.

**MUSTARD SAUCE**
1 cup / 250 ml. sour cream
2 tbsp. mustard
1 tsp. sugar
Salt
1 hard-boiled egg (sliced)
Chopped parsley

To make the sauce, mix the sour cream, mustard, sugar, and salt. When the fish is ready, allow to cool slightly, place in the center of a serving plate, and cut into ³/₄-inch slices (2 cm.). Rearrange in the shape of a fish and add the head for decoration. Decorate the plate with slices of hard-boiled egg surrounding the fish, drizzle the mustard sauce over the fish, and sprinkle with parsley.

# MACKERELS IN OIL
## (scrumbii in ulei)

This dish is traditionally prepared in the summer and then kept for the winter to be eaten as a snack or light meal.

Salt
2 lb. / 1 kg. mackerel fillets
3-4 lemons
2 bay leaves
5-6 peppercorns
2 tsp. salt
Oil

Salt the fillets and leave for 1 hour. Add the juice of the lemons and leave another 20-30 minutes. Now place the fillets, one by one, inside a jar, in a row. Once one layer is done, add a bay leaf, 2-3 peppercorns, salt and a little lemon juice and oil. Continue until the fillets are all in the jar. Add a 1¼-inch layer (3 cm.) of oil and cover the top with some plastic wrap. Fill a deep pot with water and bring to the boil. Lower the jar into it and cook the fish 20-30 minutes. Allow to cool and serve cold.

## GRILLED MACKERELS WITH HOT SAUCE
### (scrumbii la grătar cu sos picant)

Romanians usually have these for lunch with a green salad and dark crusty bread.

> **12 fresh mackerels**
> **Coarse sea salt**
> **5 tbsp. olive oil**
> **2 large red bell peppers**
> **2 small chili peppers**
> **Juice of 1 lemon**
> **Salt**
> **Pepper**

Wash the mackerels, sprinkle with sea salt, and refrigerate 2-3 hours. Then wash the fish in cold water, dry, and score the skin 3-4 times on each side. Brush grill with 3 tbsp. olive oil and grill the mackerels 4 minutes on each side. The fish should become firm and the skins golden brown.

To make the sauce, dice all the peppers. In a saucepan, simmer them with lemon juice over medium heat for 5 minutes, until they soften. Transfer to a food processor and mix briefly with remaining olive oil and salt and pepper, until the sauce is smooth. Allow to cool completely.

# FRIED COD IN TOMATO SAUCE
## (mîncare de cod cu roşii)

4 tbsp. vegetable oil or butter
1 large onion (coarsely chopped)
2 tbsp. flour
½ salt
½ tsp. sugar
4 peppercorns
1 bay leaf
2 cans tomatoes
2 lb. / 1 kg. cod fillets

In a pan containing 2 tbsp. heated oil, cook the onion until golden. Add ½ tsp. flour, the salt, sugar, peppercorns, bay leaf, and tomatoes. Bring to the boil, then simmer on low heat another 15 minutes. Cut the cod into 2¼-inch pieces (6 cm.), cover in the remaining flour, and fry in a clean pan containing the remaining oil, on medium heat, 5 minutes on each side. Pour the tomato sauce into a shallow casserole dish and place the pieces of fried fish over the sauce. Bake at 350 degrees (180 degrees C) for 30 minutes. Serve with rice or mămăligă (see recipe).

# STURGEON GRATIN WITH MUSHROOMS
## (morun gratinat cu ciuperci)

Sturgeons are plentiful in Romania's waters. This fish has a darker meat than cod, for example, and a moderately firm texture. Carp or trout can be substituted for sturgeon in these two recipes.

**2 lb. / 1 kg. sturgeon fillet**
**1 large onion (chopped)**
**3 bay leaves**
**¼ cup / 60 ml. white wine**
**Salt**
**Pepper**
**Water to cover**
**2 eggs (separated)**
**½ cup / 125 g. butter**
**½ cup / 125 g. flour**
**1 cup / 250 ml. milk**
**¼ cup / 60 ml. sour cream**
**¼ cup / 60 g. grated caschcaval or provolone**
**cheese**
**2 tbsp. breadcrumbs**
**1 cup / 250 g. sliced button mushrooms**

Cut the fish into 6 slices and place in a pot with the onion, bay leaves, wine, salt, and pepper. Add enough water to cover and simmer on medium heat for 15 minutes. Whisk the egg whites and set aside for the sauce. In a small saucepan, melt the butter over medium heat. Mix the flour, milk, sour cream, and 1 tsp. salt. Add mixture to butter. Whisk continuously until the sauce begins to thicken, then remove from heat and allow to cool slightly. Then add half the caschcaval and egg yolks and fold in the egg whites. Butter a baking pan and sprinkle the bottom with breadcrumbs. Carefully arrange the fish slices in the pan, cover with half the sauce, add the mushrooms, then cover with the remaining sauce. Sprinkle the remaining caschcaval over the sauce and bake at 350 degrees (180 degrees C) for 15 minutes. Serve with boiled potatoes or buttered green beans.

# FISHERMAN'S STURGEON
## (morun pescăresc)

---

2 lb. / 1 kg. whole sturgeon
Salt
½ cup / 125 ml. oil
3 cloves garlic (chopped)
2 sprigs thyme
Pepper
2 red bell peppers (chopped)
4 large tomatoes (chopped)
2 tbsp. tomato paste
4 tbsp. white wine
2 tbsp. chopped parsley

Cut the fish into 6 pieces, wash, and salt. Place in a baking pan and drizzle with half the oil. Add the garlic, thyme, and pepper and bake at 350 degrees (180 degrees C) for 15 minutes. Remove from the oven and add the peppers, tomatoes, and tomato paste. Drizzle with remaining oil and bake again for 30 minutes. Add the wine for the last 15 minutes of cooking. Serve hot or cold, sprinkled with parsley.

# RUSSIAN-STYLE TROUT
## (păstrăv à la russe)

2 large carrots
1 large onion
3 celery stalks
2⅛ cups / ½ l. water
2 tbsp. vinegar
Salt
1 tsp. pepper
3 lb. / 1½ kg. trout
4 tbsp. mayonnaise
2 tbsp. chopped parsley

Chop all the vegetables and add to a pot with the water. Add the vinegar, salt, and pepper. Bring to the boil and simmer 5 minutes on medium heat. Add the trout and simmer another 10 minutes. Allow the fish to cool, then peel off skin. Serve trout cold with Russian Salad (see recipe), mayonnaise, and sprinkled parsley.

# FISH-STUFFED TOMATOES
## (roşii umplute cu peşte)

12 medium tomatoes
1½ lb. / 750 g. cod or salmon fillet
2 onions (quartered)
2 tbsp. white rice (cooked and cooled)
1 tbsp. butter
2 tbsp. chopped dill
2 tbsp. chopped parsley
½ tsp. salt
½ tsp. pepper

Cut the tops off the tomatoes and hollow tomatoes out. In

a food processor, combine the fish, onion, rice, butter, herbs, salt, and pepper. Pulse 5-6 times to combine, then fill the tomatoes with the mixture. Arrange the tomatoes in a deep pan.

**SAUCE**
**½ onion (diced)**
**1 tbsp. butter**
**½ tsp. flour**
**2 cans tomatoes**
**1 tsp. sugar**
**½ tsp. salt**
**1 tbsp. chopped parsley**

To make the sauce, cook the onion in butter until softened, then add the flour and mix well. Next add the tomatoes, sugar, and salt. Simmer the sauce 15 minutes over medium heat. Add the parsley, then pour over the tomatoes. Cover the pan and simmer 30-40 minutes.

# FISH BALLS WITH PICKLE SALAD
## (chifletuţe din peşte cu salată de castraveţi)

1 cup / 250 ml. white-wine vinegar
2 tbsp. sugar
Salt
7 oz. / 200 g. pickles (chopped)
5 green onions (chopped)
1 small chili pepper (minced)
2 tbsp. coriander (chopped)
1 tbsp. grated lemon peel
2 tbsp. lemon juice
4 cloves garlic
1 tsp. ground ginger
2 lb. / 1 kg. cod fillet
2 eggs
½ tsp. pepper
4 tbsp. flour
2 tbsp. olive oil

In a saucepan, make the salad by heating the vinegar, sugar, and 1 tsp. salt until the sugar dissolves. Cool, then add the pickles, half the green onions, half the chili pepper, and half the coriander. Mix well and set aside. In a food processor, chop the rest of the green onions, chili pepper, and coriander, as well as the lemon peel, lemon juice, garlic, and ginger. Mix until it becomes a purée. To the mixer, add the cod, eggs, salt, and pepper and homogenize. Using wet hands, roll the mixture into 1½-inch balls (4 cm.). Roll through the flour and fry in hot olive oil, about 5 minutes. Serve the fish balls on top of the pickle salad.

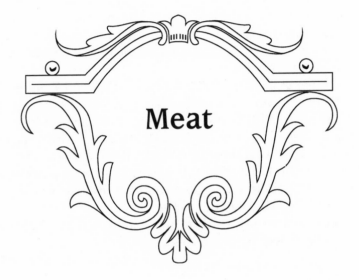

# Meat

As a little girl, whenever I would spend the night at my grandparents' home, I would hear *basme*, or fairy tales. These stories had as their main heroes Făt Frumos (Prince Charming, always depicted on a white horse) and Ileana Cosinzeana, the most beautiful girl in the land, with blue eyes and blond hair so long it touched the ground.

One of the stories always told to me was how Făt Frumos went away to fight the evil dragon. Ileana went up to the top of a mountain and cried so much that her tears formed the river now known as the Siret, which flows through the Carpathian Mountains.

Another story depicts the feast of 7 days and 7 nights that Făt Frumos's father, the king, threw to celebrate the slaying of the dragon and Făt Frumos's marriage to Ileana. All the king's subjects, as well as royalty from 70 countries, joined the celebrations. Food was served in golden dishes and included partridge, venison, fish, fruits in honey, and exotic pastries and cakes. They say that the sound of the festivities was so great that for 7 days the sun did not set.

I have gathered in this chapter some favorite Romanian meat dishes worthy of a fairy-tale feast.

# CHICKEN WITH QUINCES
## (găină cu gutui)

My grandfather had a friend who had a farm nearby and he would provide meat for the family. Granddad would take us along on his visits to the farm to make sure that we modern children got in touch with nature and learned to love animals. I quickly befriended some of the animals, and I would learn to recognize them whenever I returned. There were ducks, chickens, and roosters, all living happily together. I would give them names and feed them. Of all the birds in the yard, only one would not become my friend—the turkey. He was proud and nasty and did not allow me to pet him, emitting horrible guttural screeches when I came near.

I once found out the danger of wearing red in front of him (which was my favorite color as a little girl). The reaction to my red sweater was a swift turkey attack, as he ran and bit down into my skirt. Luckily enough, my grandfather noticed and came to the rescue, but I am sure that my screams were heard for miles around!

Maybe it's no accident that I've stayed away from turkey recipes in this cookbook. Here are some chicken dishes to enjoy instead.

> **6 pieces chicken**
> **3 tbsp. butter or margarine**
> **2 tbsp. flour**
> **Salt**
> **Water to cover**
> **4 quinces**
> **2 tsp. sugar**

In a deep pan, cook the chicken in 1 tbsp. butter until the meat starts to brown. Then add ½ tbsp. flour, the salt, and enough water to cover the chicken. Cover and simmer on medium heat for 20 minutes. Meanwhile, peel the quinces and cut them into thick slices, removing the seeds. (If quinces are not available, apples make a nice alternative.) Cover the slices in the remaining flour and cook them in a separate pan on medium heat, in the remaining butter, until brown on both sides. When the meat is almost cooked, add the sugar to the liquid and arrange the quinces over the chicken. Cover the pan again and simmer until the sauce has thickened, about 10 minutes, shaking the pan from time to time.

# FRIED CHICKEN WITH GARLIC SAUCE
## (pui la tavă cu mujdei)

---

6 chicken legs
3 tbsp. butter (melted)
Salt
Pepper
½ cup / 125 g. garlic cloves
2 cups / 500 ml. beef stock

Brush the chicken legs with butter, salt, and pepper and cook in a hot pan for 10-15 minutes, turning when brown. Meanwhile make the sauce by processing the garlic into a paste, then adding the stock and 1 tsp. salt. When the chicken is almost ready, pour the sauce over the meat and simmer over medium heat another 10 minutes. Serve the chicken next to mămăligă (see recipe) drizzled with garlic sauce.

# CHICKEN AND SAUSAGE CASSEROLE
## (caserolă cu pui şi cârnaţi)

½ lb. / 250 g. sausages (sliced)
2 large onions (sliced)
6 tbsp. olive oil
2 lb. / 1 kg. chicken wings and drumsticks
½ lb. / 250 g. button mushrooms
5 cloves garlic (crushed)
5 tbsp. flour
2½ cups / 625 ml. chicken stock
1 cup / 250 ml. red wine
3 tsp. salt
1 tsp. pepper
3 sprigs fresh thyme
3 bay leaves

In a large and deep frying pan, cook the sausages and onions on high heat in the olive oil about 6 minutes, until they begin to brown. Remove from the pan and set aside. In the remaining oil, cook the chicken 10 minutes on medium heat. Then add the whole mushrooms and garlic and cook another 5 minutes. Now return the sausages to the pan, add the flour, and stir continuously until all the ingredients are well coated. Add the chicken stock, red wine, salt, pepper, thyme, and bay leaves. Mix well and bring the liquid to the boil. Lower the heat, cover the pan, and simmer another 5-10 minutes, until the sauce thickens. Serve with white rice.

# ROAST DUCKLINGS ON SWEET CABBAGE
## (boboc de raţă pe varză dulce)

Two 5-lb. / 2½-kg. ducklings (thawed if frozen)
Salt
2 medium red cabbages
Butter or margarine
2 tbsp. chicken stock
2 tsp. paprika
2 tbsp. ketchup
3 tbsp. sugar
Pepper
Crushed garlic
Thyme

Clean out the ducklings and sprinkle with salt. Leave for 1 hour. Meanwhile, cut the cabbages into thin strips and cook in 4 tbsp. butter on medium heat with the stock, paprika, ketchup, sugar, and a pinch of salt and pepper. Cook until the cabbage is soft. Place in the bottom of a roasting pan, arranging in a uniform layer to cover the whole surface. When the ducklings are ready, wipe all the liquid off them with paper towels, then rub their skins with butter, garlic, and thyme. Place on the cabbage and roast in the oven at 325 degrees (170 degrees C) for 2 to 2½ hours, until the ducklings have golden skins. (Baste the birds regularly and turn them over halfway through the cooking time.) Serve on a large dish, with the ducklings placed over a bed of the cabbage, surrounded by roasted new potatoes.

# ROAST DUCKLINGS
# WITH BAKED APPLES
## (friptură de rață cu mere coapte)

**Two 5-lb. / 2½-kg. ducklings (thawed if frozen)**
**Salt**
**14 large green apples**
**Paprika**
**4 cloves garlic (crushed)**
**Pepper**
**1 tbsp. oil**
**2 tbsp. water**

Clean out the ducklings, then wash and salt them. Dry with paper towels and insert 2 peeled apples into each body cavity. Then sprinkle the ducklings with paprika, garlic, salt and pepper. Drizzle the oil into a roasting pan and place the ducklings in the pan. Roast at 325 degrees (170 degrees C), basting with the juice in the pan. After about 45 minutes, place the remaining apples in the pan around the ducklings and roast another 45 minutes. Remove the apples and allow the ducklings to finish cooking, about 30-60 minutes.

When the ducklings are ready, carve the meat and arrange in the center of a serving dish. Surround the duck with the baked apples. Transfer the juice in the roasting pan to a small saucepan. Add the water and simmer about 5 minutes. Then pour the sauce over the duck.

# PARTRIDGE PILAF
## (pilaf de potirnichi)

Although partridge has a distinct flavor compared to more commonly used birds, small chickens can be used for this recipe.

> 3 young partridges
> Salt
> 1 tsp. paprika
> 2 tsp. chopped rosemary
> Water to cover
> 4 tbsp. butter or margarine
> 2 cups / 500 ml. white rice
> 3 cloves garlic (crushed)
> Chopped parsley

Cut the partridges into pieces or ask your butcher to prepare it. Place in a large deep pan and sprinkle with salt, paprika, and rosemary. Add enough water to cover the meat. Simmer for 15 minutes on medium heat and remove any foam that forms. In a second large pan, fry the rice and butter until the rice appears to be dry. Now add the meat to the pan containing the rice, as well as 2 ladles of cooking liquid from the first pan. Add the garlic and some parsley. Bring to the boil, transfer to an ovenproof casserole dish, and bake at 350 degrees (180 degrees C) until the rice is completely cooked, about 30 minutes.

# CLUJ-STYLE VEAL CUTLETS
## (antricot de vită clujean)

Cluj was once the Hungarian capital of Transylvania. Opinions vary about the city's true ownership, as the Germans founded it for a Hungarian king, but Romanians feel that it is without a doubt theirs. It is best known for its café society and literary past and still is a university center. The paprika in this recipe may be the clue to its origins.

> 6 boneless veal cutlets
> 4 tbsp. flour
> 4 tbsp. oil
> 2 cups / 500 ml. beef stock
> 1 large onion (sliced)
> 2 tsp. paprika
> 1 lb. / 500 g. button mushrooms (sliced)
> 2 tbsp. butter
> ½ lb. / 250 g. canned whole carrots
> 4 large tomatoes (sliced)
> 3 tsp. salt
> 1 tsp. pepper
> 4 tbsp. white wine
> 3 tbsp. chopped parsley

Pound each cutlet to flatten, then flour both sides. In a deep frying pan mix half the oil with 5 tbsp. stock and put the floured cutlets in the liquid. In a saucepan over medium heat, simmer the onion with the remaining stock and oil and the paprika for 15 minutes. Pour the sauce over the cutlets and simmer about 40 minutes. Halfway through cooking, add the mushrooms and butter. Five minutes before the end of cooking add the whole carrots, tomatoes, salt, pepper, white wine, and parsley. Serve hot with boiled potatoes.

# MURESH-STYLE GOULASH
## (gulaş mureşan)

Here is another recipe with Hungarian influence, from a town called Tîrgu Mureş, near Cluj. It was once a great Magyar city, at the heart of the meadows, forests, and valleys that make up Transylvania. Dishes from this region are distinctively spicier than those from other regions of the country.

2 large onions
3 large carrots
2 large red bell peppers
4 tbsp. chopped celery leaves
2 tsp. paprika
2 tbsp. tomato paste
3 cups / 750 ml. beef stock
1 lb. / 500 g. veal stew meat
1 tsp. ground cumin
3 tsp. salt
5 large potatoes (cubed)
2 large eggs
½ cup / 125 g. flour
½ cup / 125 g. whole button mushrooms
3 cloves garlic (crushed)
1 tsp. pepper
½ chili pepper (chopped)
2 tbsp. chopped parsley

Slice the onions, carrots, and peppers and place in a large pot. Add the celery leaves, paprika, tomato paste, and stock. Bring to the boil, then add the cubed meat, cumin, and 2 tsp. salt and simmer for 2 hours on medium-low heat. Next add the cubed potatoes and bring to the boil again. Meanwhile use the eggs, flour, and 1 tsp. salt to make a batter for zdrenţe (see Romanian Soup Noodles recipe) and add to the goulash when it begins to boil. Finally add the mushrooms, garlic, pepper, chili, and half the parsley and simmer gently, on medium-low heat, 30 minutes more. Serve hot, sprinkled with the remaining parsley.

## POLISH VEAL STEW
(tocană de vițel poloneză)

---

**1 lb. / 500 g. veal stew meat**
**½ cup / 125 ml. oil**
**Water**
**3 large onions (sliced)**
**⅔ cup / 90 g. flour**
**2 tsp. salt**
**1 tsp. pepper**
**2 tsp. garlic powder**
**1 cup / 250 g. white bread**
**2 eggs**
**3 tbsp. chopped parsley**

Cover the veal cubes in 2 tbsp. oil and 2 tbsp. water. In a large saucepan, simmer the onions with 4 tbsp. oil and 4 tbsp. water on high heat for 5 minutes. Dissolve 2 tbsp. flour in 2 tbsp. water and add to the onions, stirring until it begins to thicken, about 5 minutes. Then add 6 cups water (1½ l.), the salt, pepper, and garlic powder. Bring to the boil, then simmer 30 minutes on medium heat. Pour the sauce over the veal and continue simmering together another 30 minutes. In a small bowl, mix together the bread, eggs, remaining flour, and salt. Use the batter to form small balls and add to the hot sauce. Simmer another 15 minutes. Serve hot, sprinkled with parsley.

# STUFFED PEPPERS
## (ardei umpluți)

---

¾ lb. / 375 g. ground veal or beef
½ cup / 125 g. white rice
2 tsp. salt
3 tsp. pepper
1 egg
3 tbsp. chopped parsley
4 tbsp. cold water
12 large green bell peppers
2 tbsp. flour
Boiling water
1 large onion (chopped)
2 large carrots (chopped)
4 tbsp. chopped celery leaves
4 tbsp. oil
2 cups / 250 ml. water
4 tbsp. tomato paste
2 tsp. sugar
4 large tomatoes (chopped)

In a large bowl, mix together the meat, rice, salt, 2 tsp. pepper, egg, half the parsley, and the 4 tbsp. cold water. Cut the tops off the peppers, wash out any seeds, and fill with the meat mixture. When filled, dip the tops of the peppers in flour. Grease a baking pan and sit the peppers in it. Cover the bottom of the pan with boiling water and bake peppers at 350 degrees (180 degrees C) for 30 minutes. To make the sauce, mix the onion, carrots, and celery leaves in the oil and 2 cups water. Heat in a saucepan until it begins to boil, then add the remaining flour, pepper, tomato paste, and sugar. Simmer 20 minutes over low heat, then pass through a sieve and pour over the peppers. Continue baking the peppers for 15 minutes, then add the tomatoes and cook another 5 minutes. Serve hot with mămăligă or potatoes.

# STUFFED WHITE CABBAGE
## (sarmale cu varză)

1 large white cabbage
2 onions (chopped)
2 tbsp. white rice
1½ lb. / 750 g. ground beef or veal
1 tbsp. chopped parsley
Salt
Pepper
6 tomatoes
2 tbsp. tomato paste
Juice of ½ lemon
3 cloves garlic (chopped)

Break off the cabbage leaves and cut out the hard spines with a knife. Boil a pot of salted water and add the leaves, simmer several seconds, and remove when they begin to soften. Place the cabbage leaves on paper towels and allow to cool. In a greased frying pan, brown the chopped onions and rice, then add ½ cup (125 ml.) hot water. Cover and allow the rice to swell, then cool several minutes. In a bowl, mix together the meat, rice, parsley, salt, and pepper. On a wooden board, lay out a cabbage leaf, and crossing over the part that was cut out, add a spoonful of meat mixture, fold in the sides, and roll the leaf over the meat to form a sausage shape. Repeat with the rest of the leaves and meat. Roll up the small remaining cabbage leaves and cut into strips. Slice up the tomatoes.

In a large casserole dish, place several tomato slices in the bottom, half of the shredded cabbage, and a tight layer of stuffed cabbage. Cover with another layer of tomato and stuffed cabbage, and cover with the remaining tomato slices and shredded cabbage. Dilute the tomato paste in 4 cups water (1 l.), add the lemon juice and garlic, and pour over the cabbage. Cover and bake 1 hour at 325 degrees (170 degrees C). Add more diluted tomato paste if the liquid lowers to half its original level. Serve hot with mămăligă and sour cream.

# ROMANIAN BEEF STEW
## (tocană de carne)

2 lb. / 1 kg. beef
2 tbsp. butter or margarine
5 onions (chopped)
5 tomatoes
4 celery stalks (chopped)
2 cloves garlic (chopped)
2 red bell peppers (chopped)
Salt
Pepper

Cut the meat into cubes and fry in the butter for several minutes. Now add the onions and fry 5 minutes. Add several tablespoons of water and continue to simmer over medium heat, adding water if necessary, until the meat is cooked (20 minutes). Peel the tomatoes and remove the seeds. Cut tomatoes into small pieces and add to the meat, along with the celery, garlic, peppers, salt, and pepper. Cover the pan and simmer on low heat for 15 minutes. Serve with mămăligă.

# MEAT AND GREEN BEAN STEW
## (fasole verde cu carne)

1½ lb. / 750 g. beef
2 tbsp. butter or margarine
2 onions (chopped)
½ tbsp. flour
Hot water to cover
Salt
2 lb. / 1 kg. fresh green beans (broken in half)
⅔ cup / 150 ml. tomato purée
2 tbsp. chopped parsley
2 tbsp. chopped chives

Cut the meat into equal cubes and fry in the butter over high heat in a deep pan, about 10 minutes. Add the onions and fry 2-3 minutes. Add the flour and mix well. Now add enough hot water to cover the meat, add salt, and simmer slowly for 30 minutes. Add the green beans and simmer 15 minutes more. Add the tomato purée, parsley, and chives. Transfer to the oven and bake at 350 degrees (180 degrees C) for about 30 minutes, until a rich sauce has formed around the meat.

## BEEF GHIVECH
### (ghiveci cu carne de vacă)

1½ lb. / 750 g. beef
3 tbsp. butter or margarine
2 large onions (chopped)
2 cloves garlic (chopped)
Salt
Warm water to cover
1 carrot
2 large red bell peppers
1 large aubergine (eggplant)
1 large courgette (zucchini)
7 oz. / 200 g. green beans
1 small cauliflower
3 potatoes
1 celery stalk
6 large tomatoes
7 oz. / 200 g. butter beans
9 oz. / 250 g. peas
3 tbsp. chopped parsley
1 bay leaf

Cut the beef into equal cubes and fry them in a pot over

medium-high heat with the butter, onions, and garlic for about 10 minutes. Add salt and enough warm water to cover the meat. Cover the pan and simmer on low heat for 1-1½ hours. Meanwhile, cut the carrot, peppers, aubergine, courgette, green beans, cauliflower, potatoes, celery, and tomatoes into small pieces. When the cooking time is up for the meat, add all the vegetables to the pot, as well as the parsley and bay leaf. Cover and simmer for 15 minutes, then transfer the pot to the oven and bake at 350 degrees (180 degrees C) for 30 minutes or until the liquid has reduced, mixing the contents of the pot from time to time.

# ROMANIAN KEBABS
## (mititei)

This dish is one of the most well known foods associated with Romanian cuisine. Summer weekends would not be the same without these. My mother leaves all the barbecuing to my father, but preparing the *mititei* is still her job. The seasonings and baking soda are the most important elements to these little kebabs, shaped like small sausages and simply grilled until they are fragrant and sizzling, and served with pickled peppers and a salad.

> **2 lb. / 1 kg. ground beef**
> **9 oz. / 250 g. suet (or shortening)**
> **Salt**
> **Pepper**
> **Pinch cumin**
> **3 cloves garlic (minced)**
> **¼ tsp. baking soda**
> **3 tbsp. beef stock**
> **Oil**

Mix the meat and suet together (easiest with your hands).

Add salt, pepper, cumin, garlic, baking soda, and stock. Make sure the baking powder is well distributed through all the meat by kneading the meat for at least 5 minutes. Place the meat in a bowl and refrigerate for 5-6 hours. Take spoonfuls of the meat and with moistened hands form into short sausage shapes about 2½ inches long (6 cm.) and ¾ inch thick (2 cm.). Brush with oil and grill for about 10 minutes.

## ROMANIAN MEATLOAF
### (ruladă de carne tocată)

2 lb. / 1 kg. ground beef
2 onions (chopped)
1 slice white bread soaked in water (crust removed)
Salt
Pepper
2 tbsp. chopped parsley
1 egg (raw)
3 eggs (hard-boiled)
2 tbsp. olive oil
1 tbsp. breadcrumbs

In a food processor, mix the meat, onions, and bread. Add the salt, pepper, parsley, and raw egg and mix again. On a clean, wet tea towel, arrange the meat in the shape of a rectangle. Place the hard-boiled eggs in a row on the meat. Pulling one side of the towel over the meat, roll the meat to enclose the eggs and pat in the ends to make them smooth. Place the meatloaf in a greased pan, drizzle with oil, and sprinkle with breadcrumbs. Bake at 350 degrees (180 degrees C) for 45 minutes. Serve in slices on a bed of lettuce or red cabbage leaves.

# MOLDAVIAN HAMBURGERS
## (pîrjoale moldoveneşti)

3 onions (minced)
1 tbsp. butter or margarine
1 lb. / 500 g. ground meat (beef, lamb, or a
    mixture)
2 slices white bread (moistened)
1 egg
Salt
Pepper
3 cloves garlic (minced)
2 tbsp. chopped parsley
2 tbsp. chopped dill
Breadcrumbs

In a small pan, cook 2 of the onions in butter until they are
golden brown. In a large bowl, mix these with the meat,
bread, and the remaining onion. Now add the egg, salt, pepper, garlic, and herbs. Mix well. Take handfuls of meat and
shape into patties. Now coat with breadcrumbs and fry in a
hot pan until golden brown on each side, about 10 minutes.
Serve with mashed potatoes, mixed vegetables, or salad.

# MARINATED MEATBALLS
## (chiftele marinate)

Ground meat mix as for Moldavian Hamburgers
2 tbsp. flour
1 small onion (coarsely chopped)
½ tsp. flour
1 tbsp. tomato paste
⅔ cup / 150 ml. water
Salt
½ tsp. sugar
3 peppercorns
1 bay leaf
2 tbsp. white-wine vinegar
2 tbsp. chopped parsley
2 tbsp. chopped dill

Form the meat mix into small balls and coat in 2 tbsp. flour instead of breadcrumbs. In a very hot pan, quickly fry the meatballs on all sides until brown. Remove the meatballs from the pan and place in a casserole dish.

To the same pan, add the onion and ½ tsp. flour. Dilute the tomato paste in the water and add it to the pan, as well as the salt, sugar, peppercorns, bay leaf, vinegar, and herbs. Gently simmer for about 5 minutes, stirring occasionally. Then pour the sauce over the meatballs and leave 1 hour at least. This is best served the next day, after allowing the meatballs to absorb the flavors of the sauce. They can be reheated in the oven.

# LAMB WITH SPINACH
## (miel cu spanac)

1 lb. / 500 g. lamb
2 tbsp. butter or margarine
1 large onion (coarsely chopped)
½ tsp. flour
3 lb. / 1½ kg. fresh spinach
1 tbsp. beef or vegetable stock
2-3 tbsp. water
Salt
Lemon juice

Cut the meat into small squares and fry over high heat in the butter until brown, about 10 minutes. Add the onion, flour, spinach, stock, water, and salt while still frying, and allow to come to the boil. Now transfer the meat and spinach to an ovenproof dish and cover. Bake at 350 degrees (180 degrees C) for 30-40 minutes. Just before serving, drizzle lemon juice over the lamb.

# TONGUE WITH OLIVES
## (limbă cu măsline)

One 2-lb. / 1-kg. cow's tongue
3 carrots (sliced)
3 celery stalks (sliced)
3 onions (chopped)
Cold water to cover
Oil
2 tbsp. beef stock
1 tbsp. white-wine vinegar
1 tsp. sugar
3 peppercorns
1 bay leaf
Salt
7 oz. / 200 g. green olives
Chopped parsley
1 lemon (sliced)

Ask your butcher to prepare the tongue for you. Wash it before beginning to cook. Place in a large pot with the carrots, celery, one of the onions, and the water and bring to the boil. Simmer on medium heat for about 30 minutes or until the tongue is nearly cooked, removing any foam that forms. When the meat is ready, remove it from the pot and cut into slices ³/₄ inch thick (2 cm.).

In a deep pan, fry the remaining onions in oil until they soften, then add the stock, vinegar, sugar, peppercorns, bay leaf, salt, and 1 cup (250 ml.) of the tongue's cooking liquid. Then add the olives and tongue, and simmer on medium heat 20 minutes. This dish can be served cold or hot, sprinkled with parsley and garnished with lemon slices.

# KIDNEYS IN WHITE-WINE SAUCE
## (rinichi cu sos de vin)

1 cow's kidney or 2 veal kidneys
Cold water to cover
3 medium onions (chopped)
1 tbsp. butter or margarine
½ tbsp. flour
2 tbsp. water
2 tbsp. chicken stock
3 tbsp. dry white wine
1 tsp. paprika
Salt
Pepper

Remove the outer skin of the kidneys. Cut down the middle into two halves and remove all the interior veins. Then cut the kidneys into thin slices and place in a large saucepan with enough cold water to cover. Bring to the boil and simmer over medium heat for about 5 minutes. Drain the slices and set aside.

In a pan, fry the onions in butter until they begin to brown, then add the flour and allow to brown some more. Add 2 tbsp. water, the stock, wine, paprika, salt, and pepper. Mix well and add the kidney slices. Simmer over medium heat for another 10 minutes. Serve with toasted baguette slices.

# COW'S LIVER PATE
## (pateu de ficat de vacă)

2 onions
12 oz. / 300 g. butter
2-3 tbsp. water
12 oz. / 300 g. cow's liver
Salt
Pickles
Hard-boiled egg slices

Cut the onions into quarters and place in a pan with 1 tbsp. butter, the water, and the liver. Fry covered over medium heat until the liver is cooked, about 20 minutes. After allowing to cool, transfer the liver and onions to a food processor along with the remaining butter and some salt, and mix until it all forms a smooth paste. Transfer the pâté to a serving plate and decorate with pickles and egg slices.

# FRIED LIVER
## (ficat prăjit)

1½ lb. / 750 g. cow's liver
2 tbsp. flour
3 tbsp. oil
2 cloves garlic (chopped)
Salt
Pepper

Wash the liver well and dry it. Then cut it into slices ¾ inch wide (2 cm.) and cover in flour. Fry the liver in a hot frying pan containing the oil and garlic, about 5-10 minutes, turning halfway through. Add salt and pepper only after the liver is done cooking. Serve with assorted vegetables.

# Side Dishes

One of the most beloved of Romanian folk songs is the *Doina*. This is a very melodic, personal, deep, and emotional song that expresses the innermost dreams and hopes of the country's inhabitants. The Doina has a touch of melancholy, and many are the stories of shepherds who play the Doina on their flutes to keep threatening wolves at bay. Other stories tell of a little girl lost in the woods who sings the Doina, and the birds join in and direct her out of the forest.

The Doina often competes with the other classic Romanian folk song, the *Ciocârlia*, which means "lark" in Romanian. In contrast to the Doina, this is a more hopeful, lively melody describing the flight of the bird high in the sky towards the sun.

Just as the Doina is the national music of Romania, so is polenta (*mămăligă*) the national side dish. Despite its simplicity, it sometimes serves as a nourishing peasant dish by itself, and steaming-hot *mămăligă* certainly is comforting on a cold winter's day. Nevertheless, even though polenta is a favorite, Romanian side dishes are varied and many.

# VEGETABLE RATATOUILLE
## (ghiveci din legume)

½ cup / 125 ml. olive oil
1 onion (chopped)
3 large carrots (chopped)
4 celery stalks (chopped)
3 tbsp. chopped parsley
½ cup / 125 ml. water
2 potatoes (cubed)
2 large red bell peppers (chopped)
1 small white cabbage (chopped)
1 cup / 250 ml. tomato sauce
1¼ cups / 300 ml. water
3 tbsp. tomato paste
1 can peas (rinsed)
1 can green beans (rinsed)
3 tsp. salt
1 tsp. pepper
2 tsp. paprika
4 tbsp. white wine

In a large saucepan, heat the oil over medium heat. Add the onion and cook until it begins to soften. Add the carrots, celery, parsley, and the ½ cup water. After 5 minutes add the potatoes, peppers, cabbage, and tomato sauce, and continue to simmer another 10 minutes. Now add the 1¼ cups water and simmer until the potatoes soften, about 15 minutes. At this stage add the tomato paste, peas, green beans. salt, pepper, paprika, and wine. Cover and simmer 15 minutes. Serve hot or cold.

# MONASTIC STEW
## (tocană călugărească)

This recipe originated in Wallachia, the south-central region of Romania. There are a number of monasteries there. One of the best known is the Cozia Monastery, built in the 14th century by Mircea the Old, who is buried within. He was Dracula's grandfather.

> ⅓ cup / 85 ml. oil
> ½ cup / 125 ml. water
> 2 tbsp. chopped parsley
> 4 tbsp. chopped chives
> 1 onion (diced)
> 4 carrots (diced)
> 4 celery stalks (diced)
> 8 oz. / 250 g. button mushrooms (sliced)
> 3 potatoes (cubed)
> ½ cup / 125 g. cup green olives (pitted)
> 2 red bell peppers (sliced)
> 1¼ cups / 300 ml. water
> 4 tbsp. white rice
> 3 tomatoes (peeled and chopped)
> 3 tsp. salt
> 4 tbsp. white wine

In a large saucepan, heat the oil and the ½ cup water. Add all the herbs and vegetables, mix well, and cook on medium heat 10 minutes. Then add the 1¼ cups water and the rice, and transfer the saucepan to the oven. Bake at 350 degrees (180 degrees C) for 15 minutes. Add the tomatoes, salt, and wine and bake another 10 minutes. Serve hot.

# BUTTERED VEGETABLES
## (legume asortate cu unt)

½ cauliflower (cut in small florets)
7 oz. / 250g. carrots (peeled and cut in strips)
7 oz. / 250g. new potatoes
2 tbsp. butter
7 oz. / 250 g. peas (canned)
½ tsp. salt
1 tbsp. breadcrumbs

Boil the cauliflower, carrots, and new potatoes together until softened, about 15 minutes. Drain. Melt the butter in a hot frying pan. Transfer the vegetables to the pan. Add the peas, salt, and breadcrumbs. Stir to coat all the vegetables with the butter and breadcrumbs, and heat through. Serve hot to accompany meat dishes.

# CARROTS WITH BUTTER AND SOUR CREAM
## (morcovi cu unt si smîntîna)

1 lb. / 500 g. carrots
1 tbsp. butter
½ tsp. salt
1 tsp. sugar
2-3 tbsp. water
½ tsp. flour
⅔ cup / 150 ml. sour cream

Wash, peel, and cut the carrots into long strips. Cook them over high heat in the butter, salt, sugar, and water for 5 minutes. Cover and simmer over medium heat until the carrots soften, about 10 minutes, adding water if necessary. Next mix the flour into the sour cream and add to the carrots. Simmer for 10 minutes until the sauce thickens. This goes well with fried fish dishes.

# BUTTERED ENDIVES AND MUSHROOMS
## (andive sote cu ciuperci)

6 Belgian endives
8 oz. / 250 g. button mushrooms (sliced)
2 tsp. salt
Water to cover
½ cup / 125 g. butter
1 cup / 250 g. sour cream

Tear each endive into 4 pieces. Boil the endives and mushrooms in salted water for 10 minutes. Drain and mix with the butter until it melts. Mix in the sour cream and serve hot.


# MARINATED CABBAGE
## (varză roşie înabuşită)

1 large red cabbage
1 small white cabbage
2 tsp. salt
4 tbsp. butter
1 tbsp. sugar
2 tbsp. white-wine vinegar
¼ cup / 60 ml. sour cream

Cut the cabbage into thin strips. Add the salt and leave cabbage to absorb salt 10 minutes. Rinse the cabbage and dry with paper towels. Melt the butter in a pan and add the cabbage. Simmer on very low heat for 30 minutes. Halfway through add the sugar, vinegar, and sour cream, stirring well. Serve warm.

# CZECH CABBAGE
## (varză cehoslovacă)

2 lb. / 1 kg. white cabbage (shredded)
1 tbsp. sugar
2 tsp. oregano leaves
2 onions (chopped)
⅓ cup / 85 ml. oil
3 tbsp. water
4 tbsp. flour dissolved in 1 tbsp. water

Boil the cabbage with the sugar and oregano until soft, about 15 minutes. Drain. In a separate saucepan, simmer the onions in the oil and water over medium heat. After 10 minutes, add the flour and mix well. Bring to the boil, then simmer over medium-low heat until the liquid thickens, about 10 minutes. Add the cabbage, stir thoroughly, and continue to simmer gently for another 30 minutes. Serve hot.

# CABBAGE WITH TAIŢEI
## (varză cu taiţei)

Taiţei (see Romanian Soup Noodles recipe)
½ cup / 125 ml. olive oil
1 large white cabbage (shredded)
2 tsp. salt
1 tsp. pepper

Cook the taiţei in boiling water, drain, mix with 1 tsp. olive oil, and set aside. In a saucepan, heat the remaining oil and cook the cabbage with the salt and pepper over medium heat until it begins to soften, about 15 minutes. Mix the taiţei and cabbage and bake at 350 degrees (180 degrees C) for 15 minutes. Serve hot.

# POTATO STEW
## (ciulama de cartofi)

1 small carrot
1 onion
4-5 large potatoes
2 cups / ½ l. water
3 tbsp. chopped parsley
⅔ cup / 150 ml. milk
2 tbsp. butter
2 tbsp. flour
1 tsp. salt

Cut the carrot, onion, and potatoes into strips. Boil in water and simmer on medium heat 30 minutes. Then add the parsley and milk. In a small pan over high heat, cook the butter and flour until it becomes golden, 5 minutes. Remove from heat and add 1 tbsp. of the vegetable cooking liquid. Add the flour mixture and salt to the vegetables, stirring well until the liquid thickens. Simmer until the liquid reduces by half, about 30 minutes, and serve hot.

# HUNGARIAN POTATOES
## (cartofi ungureşti)

1½ lb. / 750 g. potatoes
3 large onions (coarsely chopped)
3 tbsp. butter
Salt
Pepper

Boil the potatoes whole in their skins for about 30 minutes. When the potatoes are soft, cool and remove the skins. Cut potatoes into cubes. Fry the onions in the butter until brown, then add the potatoes and salt and pepper to taste. Stir to coat the potatoes in butter. Fry another 5 minutes and serve hot.

# BAKED CHEESY POTATOES
## (cartofi cu brînză la cuptor)

2 lb. / 1 kg. potatoes
⅓ cup / 100 g. butter
7 oz. / 200 g. feta cheese (sliced)
3 eggs
1 cup / 250 ml. sour cream
½ tsp. salt

Boil the potatoes whole with skins on until they are soft, about 30 minutes. Cool, peel, and cut potatoes into thin slices. Butter a baking pan, then arrange a layer of potato slices in it. Next top with a layer of cheese slices, then potato again, and so on. In a small bowl, beat the eggs into the sour cream and add salt. Pour the mixture over the potatoes. Top with pieces of the remaining butter. Bake at 350 degrees (180 degrees C) for about 30 minutes.


# CHEESE-STUFFED POTATO CAKES
## (chifteluţe de cartofi umplute cu brînză)

1 lb. / 500g. potatoes
2 tbsp. flour
1 tsp. salt
½ tsp. pepper
2 eggs
1 tbsp. chopped chives
⅔ cup / 150 g. ricotta cheese
Flour for coating
2 tbsp. butter

Boil the potatoes whole for 40 minutes, peel, and mash. Add the flour, ½ tsp. salt, the pepper, and 1 egg and mix well.

Mix the remaining salt, the other egg, and the chives with the cheese. Using moist hands, shape 1 tbsp. of the potato mixture into a patty, place 1 tsp. of the cheese in its center, cover with another patty, and pinch the border to seal the cheese in. Repeat with the rest of the mixtures. Coat the cakes in flour. Fry over high heat in hot butter about 2 minutes each side until golden brown.

## SAUERKRAUT-STUFFED POTATO CAKES
### (chifteluţe de cartofi umplute cu varză acră)

1 lb. / 500g. potatoes
2 tbsp. flour
½ tsp. salt
½ tsp. pepper
1 egg
⅔ cup / 150 ml. sauerkraut
2 tbsp. butter

Prepare as for the Cheese-Stuffed Potato Cakes, but fill with sauerkraut instead of the cheese.

## POTATO AND CARROT ROLL
### (roulade de cartofi cu legume)

2 lb. / 1 kg. potatoes
1 cup / 250 ml. milk
1 tbsp. butter or margarine
1 egg (beaten)
Salt

Peel and boil the potatoes whole until soft, about 40 minutes. Drain and mash them. Mix in the milk, butter, egg, and salt to taste.

**FILLING**
**1 lb. / 500 g. carrots**
**2 tbsp. butter or margarine**
**1 tbsp. sugar**
**½ tsp. ground nutmeg**
**Pinch salt**
**3 tbsp. water**
**1 egg (beaten)**
**Sour cream**

Peel and cut the carrots into thin strips. Cook them in the butter, sugar, nutmeg, salt, and water over medium heat until they soften, about 10 minutes.

On a clean, moist towel, spread the mashed potatoes into a uniform layer. Then spread a layer of carrots on top. Grabbing hold of one long end of the towel, fold over the two layers slowly into a roll. Place the roll on a greased cookie sheet and brush with the egg. Bake at 350 degrees (180 degrees C) until the roulade becomes firmer to the touch and browns, about 30 minutes. When ready, cut into thick slices and serve with a dollop of sour cream.

# FRIED COURGETTES IN SOUR CREAM
## (dovlecei prajiţi cu smîntină)

**6 courgettes (zucchinis)**
**1 tsp. flour**
**2 tbsp. butter**
**Salt**
**1 cup / 250 ml. sour cream**
**1 tbsp. chopped parsley**

Cut the courgettes into circles. Dry the slices with paper towels. Coat with the flour. Melt the butter in a pan and fry the slices in it over high heat, 2 minutes on each side. When the slices are golden brown on both sides, transfer them to an ovenproof dish and sprinkle some salt over them. Pour the sour cream over the courgettes and sprinkle with parsley. Bake at 350 degrees (180 degrees C) for 20 minutes. Serve hot. This dish can also be made using aubergines (eggplants).

## PEASANT-STYLE COURGETTES
### (dovlecei ţărăneşti)

6-8 courgettes (zucchinis)
½ cup / 125 g. flour
½ cup / 125 ml. olive oil
5 cloves garlic (crushed)
4 tbsp. chopped dill
2 tsp. salt
Juice of 1 lemon

Peel the courgettes and slice. Flour the slices and fry over high heat in the olive oil (leave 1 tbsp. aside) 2 minutes on each side until brown. Mix together the remaining olive oil, garlic, dill, salt, and lemon juice. Pour the sauce over the fried courgette slices. Serve hot or cold.

## GREEN BEANS WITH EGGS AND CHEESE
### (fasole verde cu ouă si brînză)

2 lb. / 1 kg. fresh green beans
2 tbsp. butter
3 eggs
Salt
Pepper
1 tbsp. flour
3 tbsp. soft goat cheese or feta cheese (crumbled)

Boil the beans in salted water until soft, about 12 minutes. Drain. Butter a shallow ovenproof dish. Pour the beans in. In a bowl, beat the eggs with some salt and pepper and the flour. Add the cheese to the eggs, then pour over the beans and mix in. Bake at 350 degrees (180 degrees C) for 30 minutes, until the eggs set and the cheese starts to melt. Serve hot.

## MASHED BUTTER BEANS
### (fasole bătută)

**1 lb. / 500 g. canned butter beans**
**3 large onions**
**3 tbsp. olive oil**
**½ tsp. paprika**
**½ tsp. crushed garlic**
**Salt**

Drain the beans and rinse in plenty of cold water. Transfer to a food processor. Mix until it forms a light purée. Chop the onions and fry in olive oil until brown, then stir in the paprika. Add the onions to the beans and mix briefly. Drizzle some of the remaining olive oil into the beans. Add garlic and salt to taste and mix briefly again. Serve with pickled vegetables to accompany roasts.

# RUSSIAN-STYLE AUBERGINES
## (mîncare de vinete preparată ruseşte)

3 aubergines (eggplants)
Salt
2 tbsp. flour
4 tbsp. olive oil
1 carrot
3 large potatoes
1 celery stalk
1 lb. / 500 g. tomatoes
2 cloves garlic (chopped)
1 cup / 250 ml. tomato sauce
1 tbsp. chopped dill
1 tbsp. chopped parsley
½ tsp. sugar
Pepper

Cut the tops off the aubergines and slice them into circles ³/₄ inch wide (2 cm.). Sprinkle the slices with salt and leave 1 hour. Next squeeze out all the water in the slices and dry them well with paper towels. Flour the slices on both sides. Fry in oil over high heat, 3 minutes per side until golden. After all the aubergine slices are fried, set them aside on a plate. Cut the remaining vegetables (except the tomatoes) into thin slices. Cook in the oil remaining in the pan, over medium heat, for 15 minutes, until all the vegetables soften.

Slice the tomatoes and arrange some of them in one layer in the bottom of a rectangular baking pan. Next add a layer of the aubergines and some of the garlic, then a layer of vegetables. Start again with tomatoes, and continue until all the vegetables are used up, topping with a layer of tomatoes. Mix the tomato sauce with the dill, parsley, sugar, more garlic, more salt, and pepper. Pour over the vegetables. Bake at 350 degrees (180 degrees C) for 30 minutes and serve hot.

# LEEKS WITH OLIVES
## (praz cu măsline)

4 leeks
4 tbsp. olive oil
½ tsp. sugar
1 tbsp. vinegar
1 tbsp. vegetable stock
Salt
Pepper
⅔ cup / 150 g. black olives

Cut the leeks into circles and boil in salted water for 10 minutes until they soften. Drain and cook in hot oil several minutes, then add the sugar, vinegar, stock, salt, and pepper. Add the olives and mix well. Bake at 350 degrees (180 degrees C) for 15 minutes to allow the flavors to blend. Serve hot.

# STUFFED RED PEPPERS
## (ardei umpluți cu orez)

3 onions (chopped)
3 tbsp. olive oil
1 cup / 250 ml. white rice
3 tbsp. water
1 carrot (grated)
1 tbsp. chopped dill
1 tbsp. chopped parsley
Salt
Pepper
12 red bell peppers
3 cups / 750 ml. tomato sauce
2 cloves garlic (crushed)

Fry the onions (set 1 tbsp. aside for later) in 2 tbsp. of the oil, then add the rice and fry until the rice begins to turn yellow. Add water and simmer over medium heat for 15 minutes until the rice begins to swell, then remove from heat. Add the carrot, dill, parsley, salt, and pepper and stir. Allow to cool 10 minutes.

Slice the tops off the peppers, clean out the seeds, and fill with the rice mixture. Cover the peppers with their tops and place in a deep pan or pot. Pour the tomato sauce around the peppers, along with the remaining olive oil, onion, crushed garlic, salt, and pepper. Cover the pot and simmer on low heat about 45 minutes or until the rice is fully cooked inside the peppers. Serve hot with meat dishes in the winter, or cold with salad in the summer.

# MUSHROOM PILAF
## (pilaf de ciuperci)

---

**1 lb. / 500 g. large button mushrooms**
**2 large onions (chopped)**
**2 cups / 500 ml. vegetable stock**
**1 cup / 250 ml. white rice**
**3 tbsp. oil**
**Salt**
**Pepper**

Clean and slice the mushrooms. Place them with the onions in a deep pan and cover with the stock. Bring to the boil and simmer 15 minutes on medium heat. In a fresh pan, fry the rice in the oil several minutes, then add the mushrooms and cooking liquid. Add salt and pepper to taste. Simmer covered over low heat until the liquid is all absorbed and the rice is cooked through, about 20 minutes. This can be served hot or cold.

# POLISH CAULIFLOWER
## (conopidă poloneză)

2 medium cauliflowers
Water to cover
2 tsp. salt
½ cup / 125 ml. butter
½ cup / 125 g. fine breadcrumbs

Cut the cauliflowers into small florets. Cover with water, add the salt, then boil until they soften, about 10 minutes. When ready, drain them and pour into a shallow dish. In a small pan, melt the butter over high heat and cook the breadcrumbs 5 minutes until they brown, then pour over the cauliflower. Serve hot.

# SEMOLINA CROQUETTES
## (crochete de griş)

2 cups / 500 ml. milk
1 cup / 250 ml. semolina
1 tsp. butter
½ tsp. salt
1 egg (beaten)
1 tsp. flour
1 tbsp. butter (for frying)

Bring the milk to the boil in a saucepan, then slowly pour in the semolina, mixing continuously so that no lumps form. Continue simmering over medium heat until it thickens to the consistency of porridge, 10-15 minutes. Remove from heat and add the butter and salt. After it cools, add the egg and mix well. Using moist hands, take tablespoonfuls of the semolina and form into croquette shapes. Cover in flour. Fry in the butter over high heat 10 minutes, turning frequently, until golden brown. Serve with roasts.

# MAMALIGA WITH CHEESE
## (mă mă ligă cu brînză )

For centuries, endless cornfields have adorned the Romanian landscape. It is no wonder that polenta became a favorite dish. At times, Romanian peasants, too poor to afford white grains, suffered from pellagra, a disease caused by vitamin B deficiency since the vitamin is not found in corn. In a balanced diet, though, cornmeal is a tasty and versatile product. Polenta is one of the most basic dishes in Romanian cookery and is called *mămăligă*. Its frequent use has resulted in many variations, but the following is one of the most classic recipes.

> **2½ cups / 600 ml. water**
> **1 cup / 250 g. cornmeal**
> **½ cup / 125 g. butter**
> **1 cup / 250 g. shredded mozzarella or ricotta cheese**

Bring the water to the boil in a large saucepan. Add the cornmeal bit by bit, stirring continuously so that no lumps form, until it reaches the consistency of porridge. (Use as much cornmeal as necessary, which may be a bit more or less than 1 cup.) Mix in the butter, remove from heat, and put big spoonfuls into bowls. Sprinkle with cheese and serve immediately.

# BAKED MAMALIGA
## (mămăligă la cuptor)

When I was young, I distinctly remember seeing my grand-father prepare a tasty dish in the winter. A big lump of cooked polenta was filled with salted, tangy cheese and then placed in the oven to set and become golden brown. For some reason, which is still unclear to me today, this dish is called an *ours* (a bear). It's splendid food for a cold weekend afternoon, accompanied by a glass of milk and a good book. Here is my version.

2½ cups / 600 ml. milk
1 cup / 250 g. cornmeal
1 cup / 250 g. soft goat cheese
¾ cup / 200 g. butter or margarine
Pinch salt
3 eggs (beaten)
3 tsp. melted butter

Bring the milk to the boil in a large saucepan. Add the corn-meal bit by bit, stirring continuously so that no lumps form, until it reaches the consistency of porridge. (Use as much cornmeal as necessary, which may be a bit more or less than 1 cup.) Add half the cheese, half the solid butter, and the salt and mix well. After allowing the polenta to cool slightly, mix in the eggs. In a greased 11-inch (28-cm.) round cake pan, place half of the polenta mixture. Cover with sprinklings of the rest of the cheese as well as the remaining solid butter in small pieces. Fill the pan with the rest of the polenta and driz-zle melted butter over the top. Bake at 400 degrees (200 degrees C) for 30-40 minutes. Cut into wedges and serve hot.

# CHEESE DUMPLINGS
## (papanaşi fierti)

1 cup / 250 g. ricotta cheese
2 eggs (separated)
3 tbsp. flour
½ tsp. salt
2 tbsp. butter
Flour (for rolling)

Mix the cheese and egg yolks together. Beat the egg whites until they form soft peaks, then mix with the flour and salt. Fold the egg whites into the cheese mixture. On a wooden board, sprinkle some flour and turn out the mixture. Shape into a long roll and cut into pieces of 1¼ inches (3 cm.). Bring a pot of salted water to the boil, drop in the pieces of pastry, and boil until they all come to the surface, about 5 minutes. Drain and coat with the butter. Serve immediately.


# PEPPERS PICKLED IN VINEGAR
## (gogoşari in oţet)

4 green bell peppers
1⅓ cups / 350 ml. white-wine vinegar
⅔ cup / 150 ml. water
½ tbsp. salt
1 tbsp. sugar
½ tbsp. honey
3 bay leaves
½ tsp. cloves

Cut each pepper lengthwise into 5 solid pieces and place in a 2-cup (½-l.) jar. In a large saucepan, heat the remaining ingredients. Bring to the boil and simmer on medium heat 10 minutes. Allow to cool slightly and pour into jar. Seal the jar and leave for 2 days, after which the cover can be removed. If the level of liquid has fallen, fill with more vinegar. Cover with a cloth tied with a string and store on a cool shelf.

## PICKLED STUFFED PEPPERS
### (ardei umpluți cu zarzavat)

Baby-sized peppers are needed for this recipe but not the small hot kind. If these are not available, use the larger type but only 2 to fit this size jar.

> **4 small green peppers**
> **½ white cabbage (shredded)**
> **3 carrots (shredded)**
> **2 celery stalks (shredded)**
> **⅓ cup / 100 ml. white-wine vinegar**
> **1¾ cups / 650 ml. water**
> **2 cloves garlic**
> **1 tbsp. chopped dill**

Cut the tops off the peppers, clean out the seeds, and prick the bases with a fork. Fill each pepper with a mixture of the other vegetables. Place the stuffed peppers in 2-cup (½-l.) jar. In a saucepan bring the vinegar and water to the boil, then simmer on medium heat 10 minutes. Allow to cool, then pour into the jar, along with the garlic cloves and dill. Seal the jar and store on a cool shelf.

# SMALL PICKLES
## (castraveți mici in oțet)

2⅓ cups / 600 ml. water
⅓ cup / 100 ml. white-wine vinegar
3 bay leaves
½ tsp. cloves
1 tsp. salt
12 oz. / 400 g. small cucumbers
1 tbsp. chopped dill
3 cloves garlic (sliced)

Boil the water, vinegar, bay leaves, cloves, and salt for 10 minutes. Reduce heat to medium and simmer about 20 minutes to allow the volume to reduce. Cool slightly. Wash the cucumbers, put into a 2-cup (½-l.) jar, add the dill and garlic, and fill with as much of the warm vinegar and water as will fit. Seal the jar and allow to cool completely. When cold, add more vinegar if necessary, cover with a cloth tied with a string, and store on a cool shelf.

# Romanian Puddings (Budinçi)

In the north of Romania (Moldavia) is the Cheile Bicazului (Keys of Bicaz), a very steep winding road leading to a high mountain settlement called Lacul Roşu (Red Lake). The lake is said to be reddish in color from the brilliant sun.

When my mother was 9 years old and her sister 5, the family trekked up to Lacul Roşu on foot, a trip that my mother describes as having been both breathtakingly beautiful and full of trepidation. Looking over the edge of the footpaths was an act of bravery, the drops being so long. Nevertheless, the fresh air scented with pine made it worth the effort.

Romanians love the outdoors and take many nature trips such as this, during which they picnic with salami, cheeses, pickles, and vegetables. It all tastes even better after a long walk in fresh air. The best part of the meal for my mother and aunt would be the desserts, and often this was a slice of *budincă*. Some of these are presented below, starting with the savory ones and following with the child's favorite—the sweet *budincă*.

# POTATO AND CHEESE BUDINCA
## (budincă de cartofi şi brînză)

Romanian puddings are traditionally cooked in a bombe or large pudding dish, deep and rounded at the bottom. A large soufflé dish can also be used.

> 1½ lb. / 750 g. potatoes
> 1 tbsp. butter (melted)
> 1 tsp. salt
> 1 tsp. sugar
> ⅓ cup / 100 ml. milk
> 3 eggs (separated)
> 1 tbsp. flour
> ⅔ cup / 150 g. shredded mozzarella or crumbled
>    soft goat cheese
> Breadcrumbs

Peel the potatoes, then boil and mash them. In a large bowl, to the potatoes add the hot butter, salt, sugar, and milk and blend. Now mix in the egg yolks and flour. In a separate bowl, beat the egg whites until they are stiff. Fold into the potato mixture. Carefully blend in the cheese. Butter a dish, coat the bottom with breadcrumbs, and pour the mixture in. Bake at 350 degrees (180 degrees C) until a toothpick poked in the center comes out dry, 30-40 minutes. Serve hot.

# SPINACH PANCAKE BUDINCA
## (budincă cu spanac)

Some of these puddings use "bain marie" cooking, a French term for cooking in a hot water bath. The dish is lowered into a wide pan containing water and all of this then goes into the oven.

3 eggs
3 tbsp. club soda
1 tsp. salt
2 cups / 500 g. flour
1 cup / 250 ml. milk
⅓ cup / 100 g. butter (melted)
⅔ cup / 150 g. cooked chopped spinach
Salt
Pepper
Sour cream

Beat the eggs in a large bowl and mix in the club soda, the 1 tsp. salt, and flour. Now add milk bit by bit until you get a fairly thin pancake batter. In a large, hot, greased pan, pour some of the batter to form a round pancake about 8 inches (20 cm.) across. When bubbles appear at the surface, flip the pancake and cook until golden brown. Remove from pan and repeat with the remaining batter. Pile the pancakes up on a plate as you go along.

Grease an 8-inch (20-cm.) cake pan, place one pancake in, and brush with butter. Cover in 1-2 tbsp. spinach, season with salt and pepper, and cover with another pancake. Continue layering spinach and pancakes until you reach the top of the pan, ending with a pancake brushed with butter. Cover the pan with a plate and push down firmly. Cook the budincă "au bain marie" at 350 degrees (180 degrees C) for 30 minutes. Turn out when ready, and serve hot in slices with sour cream.

# MUSHROOM BUDINCA
## (budincă din ciuperci)

½ cup / 125 g. margarine
2 lb. / 1 kg. fresh button mushrooms (sliced)
1 large onion (chopped)
3 tsp. salt
1 tsp. pepper
1½ cups / 400 ml. boiling water
1½ cups / 400 ml. milk
½ cup / 125 g. flour
3 egg whites
1 tbsp. breadcrumbs
6 tbsp. grated caschcaval or provolone cheese

In a saucepan over medium heat, melt half the margarine and cook the mushrooms, onion, salt, and pepper for 10 minutes. Add the water and simmer on low heat for 10 minutes until the sauce reduces to form a paste. In another saucepan, warm the milk and add the remaining melted margarine and the flour, whisking so that no lumps form. Simmer over medium heat 10 minutes. Add to the mushrooms. Beat the egg whites and fold into the mushrooms. Turn this into a cake pan that was buttered and coated with breadcrumbs. Sprinkle the cheese over the top and bake at 350 degrees (180 degrees C) for about 30 minutes. Serve hot.

# MACARONI AND
# TOMATO SAUCE BUDINCA
## (budincă din macaroane cu sos tomat)

10 oz. / 300 g. macaroni
1 tbsp. olive oil
2 cups / 500 ml. tomato sauce
2 onions (sliced)
2 tbsp. chopped parsley
3 cloves garlic (chopped)
2 tsp. salt
1 tsp. pepper
3 eggs
4 tbsp. sour cream
4 tbsp. flour
2 tbsp. breadcrumbs

Cook the macaroni in salted water. Rinse in cold water, drain, and add the olive oil. Mix together the tomato sauce, onions, parsley, garlic, salt, and pepper. In a bowl, beat the eggs, then add the sour cream and flour and mix well. Line a greased dish with breadcrumbs. Add half the macaroni, then half the tomato sauce evenly over the macaroni, then the remaining macaroni. Pour over the remaining tomato sauce, then the sour cream mixture over the top. Bake 30 minutes at 350 degrees (180 degrees C) and serve hot.

# MEAT BUDINCA
## (budincă cu carne)

1 lb. / 500 g. ground beef or veal
3 tbsp. butter
2 slices white bread (soaked in water)
5 eggs (separated)
3 garlic cloves (minced)
Salt
Pepper
5 large button mushrooms
1 cup / 250 ml. beef stock
1 tbsp. flour
1 tbsp. chopped dill
2 tbsp. lemon juice

Fry the meat in 1 tbsp. butter until browned. In a bowl, mix the bread, broken into small pieces, with the meat. In a small bowl, beat 1 tbsp. butter with the egg yolks, one at a time, until smooth, then add to the meat. Season with garlic, salt, and pepper. Beat the egg whites until stiff and fold into the meat. Grease a pan or ceramic dish and fill with the meat mixture, packing it all in tightly. Place the dish in a large pan of water ("au bain marie"). Bake at 350 degrees (180 degrees C) for 45 minutes.

Meanwhile, to make the sauce, coarsely chop the mushrooms and bring to the boil in a saucepan containing the stock. Simmer on medium heat 10 minutes. Mix the remaining butter and the flour and add to thicken the sauce. Next mix in the dill and lemon juice and simmer another 10 minutes. When the budincă is ready (it should become solid like a meatloaf) turn it out onto a plate and cover with the mushroom sauce. Serve hot.

# CHICKEN-LIVER BUDINCA
## (budincă din ficat de pui)

8 oz. / 250 g. chicken livers (cubed)
½ cup / 125 ml. olive oil
3 cups / 750 ml. chicken stock
4 tbsp. flour
2 tbsp. salt
3 eggs (beaten)
2 tbsp. breadcrumbs
2 carrots (sliced)
1 onion (sliced)
2 tbsp. water
1 tbsp. mustard
1 tbsp. sugar
5 tbsp. white wine

Fry the chicken livers in ⅓ of the oil over high heat for 10 minutes. Add a few tbsp. stock mixed with 2 tbsp. flour in a saucepan and mix continuously for 1 minute. Add half the stock and all the salt, and simmer over medium heat 10 minutes until the sauce thickens. Allow the sauce to cool. To the sauce, add the eggs and livers. Pour into a greased dish lined with breadcrumbs and bake at 350 degrees (180 degrees C) for about 30 minutes. Meanwhile prepare the accompanying sauce by simmering the carrots and onion in the remaining oil and the water on medium heat for 10 minutes. Then add the remaining flour, whisking quickly to thicken the liquid, and pour in the remaining stock. Simmer on medium heat about 15 minutes. Strain the sauce to take out the carrots and onion, and mix in the mustard, sugar, and wine. Simmer over low heat for another 5 minutes. Pour over cut slices of the budincă.

# FISH BUDINCA
## (budincă cu peşte)

---

**2 lb. / 1 kg. fish fillet (cod or salmon)**
**Crusts of 2 slices white bread (soaked in milk)**
**5 eggs (separated)**
**2 tbsp. butter**
**1 large onion (minced)**
**1 tbsp. chopped dill**
**Salt**
**Pepper**

In a food processor, blend the raw fish and bread crusts. In a large bowl, add egg yolks to butter one at a time, beating after each addition. Add the fish, onion, dill, salt and pepper. Beat the egg whites until stiff and fold into the fish mixture. Pour into a buttered dish and bake "au bain marie" at 350 degrees (180 degrees C), about 30 minutes.

**BUTTER SAUCE**
**Boiling water**
**⅔ cup / 150 g. butter**
**5 egg yolks**
**Salt**
**Juice of 1 lemon**

Place a bowl over a small saucepan containing boiling water (the water should not touch the bottom of the bowl). Beat the butter slowly with an egg yolk at a time until well heated (do not allow it to boil). Add salt and lemon juice and mix well. Serve slices of the budincă covered in butter sauce.

# SALAMI BUDINCA
## (budincă cu salam)

½ cup / 125 g. margarine
½ cup / 125 g. flour
2 tsp. salt
1 tsp. pepper
2 eggs (beaten)
8 oz. / 250 g. salami (cubed)
2 potatoes (cubed and cooked)
4 tbsp. breadcrumbs

In a saucepan over medium heat, melt ¾ of the margarine. Add the flour, salt, and pepper and whisk continuously until it thickens, about 5 minutes. Cool and add the eggs, salami, and potatoes. Pour the mixture into a greased dish lined with 1 tbsp. breadcrumbs. Sprinkle the remaining breadcrumbs over the top, and bake at 350 degrees (180 degrees C) for 40 minutes.

# SOUR CREAM BUDINCA
## (budincă cu smîntînă)

6 eggs (separated)
⅓ cup / 100 g. sugar
4 tbsp. flour
1 tsp. salt
Grated peel of 1 lemon
1 tsp. vanilla extract
2 cups / 500 ml. sour cream
Fine breadcrumbs

In a bowl, mix the egg yolks, sugar, flour, salt, lemon peel, and vanilla extract. Mix in the sour cream. Beat the egg whites until stiff and fold into the mixture. Grease a pudding dish and dust with breadcrumbs. Pour in the mixture and cover the dish tightly with a plate. Bake "au bain marie" for 30 minutes at 350 degrees (180 degrees C).

**WINE SAUCE**
**3 egg yolks**
**⅓ cup / 100 g. sugar**
**1 tbsp. flour**
**2 cups / 500 ml. white wine (warmed)**

Beat the egg yolks, sugar, and flour together in a saucepan. Pour in the wine, stirring continuously. Heat over low heat, stirring, until the sauce begins to thicken, about 10 minutes. Remove from heat and continue stirring until the sauce cools. Turn the budincă out onto a plate and cover with the wine sauce. Serve warm or cold.

## WALNUT BUDINCA
### (budincă cu nuci)

---

**3 tbsp. butter**
**4 tbsp. sugar**
**2 tsp. vanilla extract**
**3 eggs (separated)**
**3 tbsp. flour**
**1 cup / 250 g. ground walnuts (soaked in 1 cup / 250 ml. milk)**
**3 tbsp. ground walnuts**
**Confectioners' sugar**

In a large bowl, beat together the butter, sugar, vanilla, and egg yolks (one at a time). Add the flour and soaked walnuts. Beat the egg whites until stiff and fold that and the rest of the walnuts into the mixture. Pour into a pudding dish dusted with confectioners' sugar, cover with a plate or lid, and bake "au bain marie" for 30 minutes at 350 degrees (180 degrees C).

**CHOCOLATE GLAZE**
**1 cup / 250 ml. milk**
**1 vanilla pod**
**5 egg yolks**
**4 tbsp. sugar**
**2 tbsp. cocoa powder**

Heat the milk and vanilla in a saucepan over high heat until boiling. Remove from heat and cover. In a bowl, beat the egg yolks and sugar. Pour into the warm milk. Cook on medium heat for 10 minutes. Keep beating throughout, until it begins to thicken and comes to the boil. Then quickly remove from heat and mix in the cocoa powder until uniform. Cover the budincă with the glaze.

# RICE AND WINE BUDINCA
## (budincă cu orez şi vin)

**1 cup / 250 g. white rice**
**4 cups / 1 l. red wine**
**1 cup / 250 g. sugar**
**⅔ cup / 150 g. butter**
**6 eggs (separated)**
**1 tsp. ground cinnamon**
**1 tsp. salt**
**Fine breadcrumbs**
**Confectioners' sugar**

In a large saucepan, boil the rice in the wine and 5 tbsp. sugar, about 20 minutes. Once cooked (the rice should be very soft and most of the wine absorbed), allow to cool. Then beat with the remaining sugar and the butter until it forms a smooth paste. Add the egg yolks one by one, mixing well. Mix in the cinnamon and salt. Beat the egg whites until stiff and fold in. Pour into a greased dish dusted with bread-crumbs. Bake 30-40 minutes at 350 degrees (180 degrees C). Turn out onto a plate and dust with confectioners' sugar when cool.

## SEMOLINA BUDINCA
### (budincă din griş)

---

2 cups / 500 ml. milk
1 tsp. vanilla extract
⅔ cup / 150 g. sugar
5 tbsp. semolina or grits
1 tsp. salt
2 tbsp. butter
3 eggs (separated)
2 tbsp. raisins
Wine Sauce (see Sour Cream Budincă)

In a saucepan over high heat, heat the milk with the vanilla and sugar. When it starts to boil, reduce to medium heat and add the semolina slowly, stirring as you go. Add the salt and continue to simmer until it thickens and forms a sort of por-ridge, about 5 minutes. Remove from heat and add the butter. Allow to cool. Add the egg yolks one at a time and the raisins. Beat the egg whites until stiff and fold in. Pour the mixture into a greased dish, cover, and bake "au bain marie" for about 40 minutes at 350 degrees (180 degrees C). Serve with Wine Sauce.

## SWEET CORNMEAL BUDINCA
### (budincă cu porumb)

---

1 cup / 250 ml. cornmeal
⅓ cup / 100 ml. flour
4 tbsp. sugar
½ tsp. salt
¼ tsp. baking powder
2 tbsp. oil
Water
5 pieces Turkish delight (chopped)
Confectioners' sugar

In a bowl, mix the cornmeal, flour, sugar, salt, baking powder, and oil. Add tablespoons of water if necessary for the mixture to become uniform. Leave to rest 10 minutes. Mix in Turkish delight. Pour into a greased and floured dish. Bake for 40 minutes at 350 degrees (180 degrees C). When cooled, dust with confectioners' sugar. Serve cold.


## APPLE BUDINCA
### (budincă cu mere)

---

3 eggs
1 cup / 500 ml. milk
1 tsp. salt
1 tsp. vanilla extract
1 loaf white bread (sliced)
6 apples (sliced)
2 tbsp. black cherries in syrup
⅓ cup / 100 ml. sugar
⅓ cup / 100 g. butter
Whipped cream or vanilla ice cream

Grease a pudding dish and dust with flour. In a small bowl beat the eggs, milk, salt, and vanilla. Cut the crust off the bread slices. Soak the bread slices in this mixture and arrange some of them around the bottom of the dish. Next arrange a layer of some apple slices in the dish. Cover with some of the cherries and some of the sugar. Add layers of bread, apples, etc., to the top of the dish, ending with bread. Pour the remaining egg and milk mixture over the bread. Dot the top of the dish with butter. Bake for 30-40 minutes at 350 degrees (180 degrees C). Serve warm with whipped cream or vanilla ice cream.

## CANDIED-FRUIT BUDINCA
### (budincă cu fructe confiate)

½ cup / 125 g. chopped crustless white bread
1½ cups / 400 ml. milk
2 tbsp. cornstarch dissolved in 1 tbsp. milk
3 eggs (separated)
1 tbsp. vanilla extract
½ cup / 125 g. chopped candied cherries or orange peel
6 tbsp. sugar
5 tbsp. white wine

Soak the bread in some cold milk, then drain. Bring the milk to the boil. Add the bread and cornstarch. Simmer 10 minutes over medium heat, stirring continuously, and leave to cool. Beat 2 egg yolks and 2 egg whites (until stiff) separately. Add these, 2 tsp. vanilla, and the candied fruits to the bread mixture. Pour into a greased pan, smooth with the back of a spoon, and sprinkle 3 tbsp. sugar over the top. Bake 30-40 minutes at 350 degrees (180 degrees C), then allow to cool. To make the sauce, place a glass bowl over a saucepan of simmering water. In the bowl, heat the remaining egg yolk and sugar until it begins to thicken, about 5 minutes. Add the wine and remaining vanilla, and whisk for 5 minutes. Serve budincă warm with the wine sauce drizzled over the top.

## SWEET CHEESE BUDINCA
### (budincă dulce cu brînză)

3 cups / 750 g. ricotta cheese
3 tbsp. sugar
2 tbsp. sour cream
1 tsp. salt
½ cup / 125 g. butter (softened)
Grated peel of 1 lemon
½ cup / 125 g. raisins
1 tbsp. flour
4 eggs (separated)
Butter Sauce (see Fish Budincă)

Mix the cheese with the sugar, sour cream, salt, butter, and lemon peel. Add the raisins, flour, and egg yolks one by one. Beat egg whites until stiff and fold in. Grease a 9-inch (22-cm.) cake pan and line with parchment paper. Pour in the mixture. Bake 40 minutes at 350 degrees (180 degrees C). Serve with sauce.

# Cakes
# and Sweet
# Loaves

Here is a tale told to me by my grandmother. It teaches a lesson about greed . . . something children always feel around sweets.

There once lived an old woman and an old man who were neighbors. Each had a daughter who was raised differently. The old woman taught her daughter to wait for riches to come her way, not to work, and to expect to be given all she desired by a rich man whom she will eventually marry. She therefore spent her days doing nothing, being very grumpy and dissatisfied with her life. The old man taught his daughter that work is good, that living modestly is all that is required, and to be happy with the simple things in life. The girl grew up content, always working happily and singing.

One day a fairy godmother dressed as a poor traveler appeared. She knocked on the old woman's door to inquire whether she could have a bed for the night. She was told that there was no room for any beggars. She then asked the same of the old man, who welcomed her in. They did not have much room, he said, but he would lay out a bed for her in the attic. The next day the traveler informed the man that she had to go but would come back for two sacks that she left in the attic. She informed him that if she was not back in three days, he had permission to give one sack to each of the girls.

Three days passed and the woman did not return. The girls happily ran up to the attic to claim their gifts. One of the sacks was shiny and new, with gold embroidery covering it. The other was old and dirty, covered in stains. The old woman's daughter immediately grabbed the new sack and declared it her own. She quickly tore it open to disappointedly find that it was completely empty. Unaffected, the old man's daughter picked up her old sack and slowly opened it. Gold coins and jewels sparkled up at her.

The old man's daughter lived a happy, modest life, helping the poor with her wealth when she could. She gave one large jewel to the other girl, making her promise that from now on she would lead a more useful life and be content with the things she was given.

The reason I was told this story as a child was to show me that having a little bit of cake now and some again later is much better than eating it all at once and ending up with a tummy ache. The story didn't help much, though, and once you taste these cakes it will become clear why.

# COOKIE TORTE
## (tort de biscuiți)

Tortes in Romanian cuisine have many variations. The torte probably originated in Germany and Hungary, but as years passed, new ones were created in Romania that reflected personal preferences. Tortes such as Othello and Napoleon have remained the same, but some of the others below are variations that my grandmother favored.

> 1 cup / 250 g. unsalted butter
> ¾ cup / 200 ml. confectioners' sugarz
> 3 eggs
> 2 tbsp. rum
> 2 tbsp. grated dark chocolate
> 8 oz. / 250 g. butter cookies (crushed)
> 1⅓ cups / 300 g. whipped cream

Beat together the butter and sugar, then the eggs one at a time. Next add the rum and chocolate. Mix in the cookie crumbs. Transfer the mixture to a floured soufflé dish, smoothing the top, and place in the freezer for at least 2 hours. When ready, carefully turn out onto a plate and cover in whipped cream.

# MERINGUE CREAM TORTE
## (tort bezea)

---

7 egg whites
⅔ cup / 150 g. sugar
2 tsp. vanilla extract
Oil

In a bowl sitting over a saucepan of simmering water, beat together the egg whites, sugar, and vanilla until you get a thick fluffy paste. Divide this into 3 equal parts and pour onto greased baking sheets that have been lined with parchment paper, spreading into 3 even 9-inch (22-cm.) circles. Bake for about 20 minutes at 300 degrees (160 degrees C) and allow to cool.

**CREAM**
1 cup / 250 ml. sugar
1 cup / 250 g. walnuts
1 cup / 250 g. unsalted butter
3 tbsp. confectioners' sugar
2 tbsp. rum

Heat the 1 cup sugar in a saucepan over medium heat for 5 minutes, until it starts to brown. Add the walnuts, stirring occasionally until they brown, about 5 minutes. Remove from heat and pour onto a greased baking sheet to cool. Then grind the nuts in a food processor. In a bowl, beat the butter with remaining sugar and the rum. Then add the ground walnuts, reserving 1 tbsp. Use the cream to cover one of the meringue rounds. Cover with another round and continue, topping the cake with a smooth layer of cream. Sprinkle with the remaining ground nuts.

# CARAMEL TORTE
## (tort caramel)

1 cup / 250 ml. sour cream
½ cup / 125 g. unsalted butter
1 tsp. vanilla extract
2 cups / 500 g. flour

In a large bowl, mix the sour cream, butter, and vanilla. Start adding the flour slowly while mixing, until you get a soft dough. Set aside for 30 minutes. Then divide the dough into 9 equal parts and roll out into round sheets to fit a 9-inch (22-cm.) cake pan. Bake each layer separately in a greased pan for 20 minutes at 350 degrees (180 degrees C). Cool completely.

### CARAMEL CREAM
⅔ cup / 150 g. sugar
1 cup / 250 ml. milk
⅔ cup / 150 g. confectioners' sugar
2 tbsp. rum
⅔ cup / 150 g. unsalted butter

Heat the sugar in a small frying pan over high heat for 5 minutes until it starts to brown, then remove from heat. In a saucepan over low heat, heat the milk, confectioners' sugar, rum, and butter for 10 minutes. Add the browned sugar and bring to the boil. When it starts to thicken (about 5 minutes), remove from heat and allow to cool. Spread the cream on 8 of the 9 cooled cake sheets and pile them up. The remaining cooled sheet is broken into rough pieces and used to top the torte. Refrigerate the torte and serve the next day.

# FAIRYTALE TORTE
## (tort poveşte)

This torte was a favorite of my grandmother's and she frequently made it for us when we were young. The result looks as though it took hard work, but it is quite simple to prepare for something so delicious.

        **5 eggs (separated)**
        **5 tbsp. sugar**
        **1 tbsp. vanilla extract**
        **2 tbsp. ground hazelnuts**
        **1 tbsp. cocoa powder**

In a large bowl, whip the egg whites with the sugar and vanilla to stiff peaks. Add the egg yolks, nuts, and cocoa powder, and fold until evenly distributed. Pour the mixture into a greased and parchment-paper-lined 11-inch (28-cm.), round, loose-bottomed cake pan. Bake at 350 degrees (180 degrees C) for about 30 minutes or until a toothpick inserted in the center comes out clean. While this layer is baking, prepare the torte's top layer.

        **TOP LAYER**
        **3 egg whites**
        **3 tbsp. sugar**
        **½ tbsp. vanilla extract**

Beat the egg whites with the sugar and vanilla to stiff peaks. When the first layer has baked, pull the oven shelf out carefully and pour this new mixture onto the baked layer. Smooth out and return to the oven. Bake 30 minutes more or until a toothpick comes out clean. Remove the torte from the pan and allow to cool.

**CREAM**
1 cup / 250 g. unsalted butter
3 tbsp. sugar
2 tbsp. cocoa powder
3 egg yolks
⅓ cup / 150 ml. whipped cream
Cherries

Whip together the butter, sugar, and cocoa powder. Add the egg yolks one at a time, beating until the cream is thick enough to coat the back of a spoon. Use this cream to cover the torte's top and sides. Decorate with swirls of whipped cream and cherries.

# OTHELLO TORTE
## (tort Othello)

9 eggs (separated)
¾ cup / 200 g. sugar
2 tbsp. cocoa powder
2 tbsp. coffee essence (see instructions below)
2 tbsp. crushed hazelnuts or walnuts
2 tbsp. flour

Beat the egg whites, adding the sugar gradually, until they form stiff peaks. Beat the yolks and fold into the whites gently. Next add the cocoa powder, coffee essence, nuts, and flour. (The coffee essence can be made by mixing 4 tbsp. instant coffee in 2 tbsp. boiling water, then allowing it to cool.) Pour the batter into a greased and parchment-paper-lined 8-by-12-inch (20-by-30-cm.) rectangular cake pan. Bake for 30-40 minutes at 350 degrees (180 degrees C) or until a toothpick inserted in the center comes out clean. When done, turn out onto a wooden board and allow to cool completely.

**CREAM**
**1 cup / 250 g. sugar**
**3 tbsp. cocoa powder**
**5 tbsp. water**
**1 cup / 250 g. unsalted butter**
**1 tbsp. rum or brandy**
**Nuts or broken pieces of chocolate**

While the torte is baking, make the cream. Mix the sugar and cocoa in a saucepan. Add the water and warm over medium heat for 10 minutes until it forms a thick paste. Allow to cool. Beat in the butter and rum until the cream is light and uniform. Cut the torte into 3 equal layers. Use half of the cream to spread between the 3 layers, and use the rest to cover the top and all sides of the torte. Decorate with nuts or broken pieces of chocolate.

# ALMOND TORTE
## (tort de migdale)

**8 eggs (separated)**
**½ cup / 125 g. unsalted butter**
**¾ cup / 200 g. ground almonds**
**2 tbsp. potato flour**
**1½ cups / 400 g. confectioners' sugar**

Beat the egg yolks and butter until light and fluffy. Add the almonds, flour, and sugar and mix well. Beat egg whites until stiff and fold in. Pour into a greased and floured 9-inch (22-cm.) cake pan and bake about 40 minutes at 350 degrees (180 degrees C), until a toothpick inserted in the center comes out clean. Turn out and allow to cool.

**GLAZE**
**Juice of 2 lemons**
**¾ cup / 200 g. confectioners' sugar**
**Whole almonds**

Beat the lemon juice and sugar until you get a foamy white cream. Cover the cooled torte with the glaze and decorate with whole almonds.

## DATE CREAM TORTE
### (tort cu curmale şi frişcă)

10 egg whites
1 cup / 250 g. confectioners' sugar
8 oz. / 250 g. pitted dates (chopped)
1 cup / 250 g. ground hazelnuts
1 tbsp. fine breadcrumbs
1 tbsp. vanilla extract
2 cups / 500 g. whipped cream
Sliced pitted dates

Beat the egg whites with the sugar to form stiff peaks. Then fold in the chopped dates, hazelnuts, breadcrumbs, and vanilla. Pour into a greased 9-inch (22-cm.) cake pan and bake at 350 degrees (180 degrees C) for about 30 minutes. When cool, cut the cake into 2 layers. Fill and cover with the whipped cream. Decorate with sliced pitted dates.

## APRICOT TORTE
### (tort de caise)

I always loved apricots as a child. The soft, furry skins and the characteristic sweet fragrance could mesmerize me. Because I loved handling them so much, I would love to help my grandmother prepare her apricot torte. She would ask me to halve them and remove the pits, a task that can usually be accomplished simply by pulling the two halves apart. Unfortunately, in an attempt to show my maturity, I would insist I could do it better using a knife. No matter how many times I was told not to use the knife, I always managed to let the knife slip and and cut a finger.

On late afternoons during the weekend, Grandma would welcome visiting family and friends and serve them her delightful tortes. We would always be fighting over who would get a second helping first, drizzled with fresh cream. My memories of these afternoons are of endless quantities of this apricot torte, enough for everybody. How is that possible with just one cake?

> ⅓ cup / 100 g. unsalted butter
> 2 tbsp. sugar
> 1 egg
> ⅓ cup / 100 g. sour cream
> 1 tsp. vinegar
> 1 tbsp. vanilla extract
> Grated peel of 1 lemon
> 1⅓ cups / 350 g. flour
> 2 lb. / 1 kg. apricots (halved and pitted)
> 3 tbsp. sugar
> Confectioners' sugar

Beat together the butter, sugar, and egg. Then add the sour cream, vinegar, vanilla, and lemon peel. Mix in the flour and refrigerate 1 hour. (You can also leave the dough overnight and continue in the morning.) Divide the dough into 2 equal parts. Roll out both pieces to the size of a 9-inch (22-cm.) cake pan, then place one piece in the greased pan and bake at 350 degrees (180 degrees C) until it starts to brown and pull away from the sides of the pan, about 30 minutes. Remove from the oven. Mix the apricots with 3 tbsp. sugar. Cover the baked torte with the sugared apricots. Place the second piece of rolled-out dough on top and return to the oven. Bake another 40 minutes or so. Allow to cool in the pan. Remove from the pan and sprinkle with confectioners' sugar.

# EVERYDAY TORTE
## (tort ieftin)

This is an unusual recipe in that it requires no baking whatsoever. Yet it results in a lovely layered torte. The dough is simple to make and very light, so that cooking each layer on the stove for several minutes only makes this a very quick dessert.

> 2 eggs
> 3 tbsp. sugar
> 1 tbsp. vinegar
> ½ tsp. baking soda (dissolved in 2 tbsp. lemon juice)
> Grated peel of 1 lemon
> 1 tbsp. vanilla extract
> 3 tbsp. oil
> 2 cups / 500 g. flour

Beat the eggs with the sugar. Mix in the vinegar, baking soda, lemon peel, vanilla, and oil until well combined. Next add flour a little at a time until you get a soft dough. Leave to rest 10 minutes. Divide the dough into 6 pieces. Roll them out into round pancakes to fit a large nonstick frying pan. Cook each one (in no grease) on both sides over low heat until brown. This should only take about 2 minutes per side. Cool.

> **CREAM**
> 1 cup / 250 g. unsalted butter
> ¾ cup / 200 g. confectioners' sugar
> 2 tbsp. coffee essence (see Othello Torte)

Beat the butter and sugar until the mixture is fluffy. Add the coffee essence. Fill and cover the cooled torte layers.

# MOCHA TORTE
## (tortă moca)

6 eggs (separated)
6 tbsp. sugar
8 tbsp. flour
1 cup / 250 g. butter
1 tbsp. vanilla extract
2 tsp. instant coffee (dissolved in 2 tbsp. hot
    water)
3 egg yolks
½ cup / 125 g. slivered almonds (toasted)

Beat the egg whites until stiff. In a separate bowl mix together the 6 egg yolks and half the sugar. Fold into the whites, along with the flour, being careful not to flatten the whites too much. Pour into a greased cake pan and bake at 350 degrees (180 degrees C) for about 30 minutes. Meanwhile, in a bowl, mix the butter, vanilla, and remaining sugar. Then add the coffee and 3 egg yolks and beat until creamy. When the torte is ready and cooled, slice in 2 and use the mocha cream to fill the center and cover the top and sides of the torte. Sprinkle with the almonds and refrigerate. Serve chilled.


# DOBOSCH TORTE
## (doboş-tort)

The Dobosch torte is a classic Hungarian dessert. Like the goulash found in both countries, it shows the importance of this western neighbor in Romanian cuisine. It's a very special cake that takes a bit of effort to get right, because of the trickiness of getting 10 layers to cook to the same consistency.

**10 eggs (separated)**
**1 cup / 250 g. confectioners' sugar**
**Juice and grated peel of 1 lemon**
**½ cup / 125 g. cake flour**

Mix the egg yolks, sugar, and lemon juice and peel until creamy. Beat the egg whites until stiff and fold into the egg yolks. Add the flour bit by bit so as not to deflate the whites. Divide the batter into 10 parts and bake each separately in a greased pan at 350 degrees (180 degrees C) for 15 minutes or just until the layers spring back when touched. Care should be taken not to overcook the layers, or they will become hard as cookies.

**CHOCOLATE CREAM**
**Boiling water**
**6 eggs**
**1 cup / 250 g. sugar**
**6 tbsp. grated dark chocolate dissolved in 4 tbsp.**
    **warm water**

While the torte layers are cooling, make the cream. Place a glass bowl over a saucepan of boiling water. Beat the eggs over the heat with the sugar until they thicken. Remove the bowl from the heat and add the chocolate. Beat well until uniform. When everything is cooled, layer the torte with the chocolate cream between each layer and over the top.

# NAPOLEON TORTE
## (tort Napoleon)

This torte originated in Lithuania. It is named after Napoleon Bonaparte because he supposedly fell in love with it when in Lithuania during his Russian campaign. It's a very rich torte because of the cream filling but nice to serve in the afternoon with coffee.

½ cup / 125 g. butter
½ cup / 125 g. sour cream
¼ tsp. baking soda
2 cups / 500 g. flour

Allow the butter to soften. Mix with the sour cream and baking soda. Next add the flour by tablespoonfuls until a batter forms that is not too dry. Divide the batter into 3 parts. Roll them out into circles to fit into a round cake pan. Place one circle in a greased cake pan, prick top with a fork, and bake about 20 minutes at 350 degrees (180 degrees C). Repeat twice with the remaining circles.

**CREAM**
5 egg yolks
½ cup / 125 g. sugar
2 tbsp. flour
1 cup / 250 ml. milk
1 vanilla pod

Beat the egg yolks with the ½ cup sugar until frothy. Mix in the flour. Bring the milk to the boil with the vanilla pod. Remove the vanilla. Add the milk to the egg yolks, mixing rapidly. Beat until the cream thickens. Leave to cool. Use the cream to sandwich the cooled torte layers.

# CHESTNUT CHARLOTTE
## (şarlota de castane)

Nuts are popular in Romanian desserts, which shows a Turkish influence. In Europe, chestnut dishes are associated with staying indoors and enjoying the warmth while the snow falls outside.

    **4 lb. / 2 kg. chestnuts**
    **¼ cup / 50 ml. water**
    **2 cups / 500 g. sugar**
    **⅓ cup / 100 ml. rum**
    **½ tbsp. vanilla extract**
    **2 tbsp. unsalted butter**
    **¾ cup / 200 g. whipped cream**

Boil the chestnuts until soft, 30-40 minutes. Discard the shells. Put chestnuts through a food processor to make a purée. Heat water and sugar on medium until sugar dissolves and forms a thick syrup, 10-20 minutes. Beat together the chestnuts and warm syrup, as well as the rum and vanilla. Next mix in the butter until you get a uniform cream. Transfer to a soufflé dish lined with plastic wrap and freeze for at least 2 hours. Turn the charlotte out on a plate when ready to serve and cover with whipped cream.

# SUMMER-FRUIT CHARLOTTE
## (şarlota de fructe)

1⅔ cups / 400 ml. fresh raspberry or strawberry
   juice
¾ cup / 200 g. sugar
9 sheets gelatin (soaked in a bowl of cold water)
2 cups / 500 g. whipped cream

Heat the fruit juice in a saucepan for 5 minutes over medium heat. Add the sugar and simmer until the sugar is completely dissolved, another 5 or 10 minutes. Remove from heat and add the gelatin sheets (discard the water). Mix well. When nearly cold, add the whipped cream. Mix again and pour into a round mold. Refrigerate for at least 2 hours. Before serving, remove the charlotte from the mold by placing it in a bowl of hot water for just a few seconds and turning it out onto a plate.


# SOUR CREAM SOUFFLÉ
## (sufleu cu smîntîn )

2 cups / 500 ml. sour cream
3 tbsp. flour
5 eggs (separated)
½ cup / 125 g. sugar
Grated peel of 1 lemon

Mix the sour cream and flour in a saucepan over medium heat, stirring all the time, until it comes to the boil, then allow to cool. In a bowl, mix the egg yolks, sugar, and lemon peel. Add to the sour cream. Beat the egg whites until stiff and fold into the sour cream mixture. Pour into a greased soufflé dish and bake for 20 minutes at 350 degrees (180 degrees C). Serve hot.

# RUSSIAN LOAF
## (chec rusesc)

1⅔ cups / 400 g. sugar
1⅔ cups / 400 g. butter or margarine
8 eggs (separated)
⅔ cup / 150 g. chopped walnuts
5 oz. / 150 g. figs (sliced)
Peel of ½ orange (in strips)
Peel of ½ lemon (in strips)
1 tsp. vanilla extract
1 cup / 250 g. flour

In a large bowl, whisk together the sugar and butter. Add the egg yolks gradually. Now add the nuts, figs, peels, vanilla, and flour. Beat the egg whites until stiff and fold in. Pour into a large greased and floured loaf pan and bake at 350 degrees (180 degrees C) for approximately 45 minutes or until the loaf pulls away from the sides of the pan and springs back when touched. Cut into squares when cooled. Serve with afternoon tea.

# BLACK CHERRY LOAF
## (chec cu vişine)

4 eggs
¾ cup / 200 ml. sugar
3 tbsp. oil
1 tbsp. vanilla extract
1 cup / 250 ml. flour
2 cups / 500 ml. drained and pitted black cherries

Beat the eggs with the sugar until fluffy. Mix in the oil and vanilla. Add the flour. Into a greased and floured loaf pan, pour one-third of the batter. Cover with half of the cherries and repeat, finishing with the remaining batter. Bake at 350 degrees (180 degrees C) for about 40 minutes or until the loaf pulls away from the sides of the pan and feels springy.

## FRUIT AND NUT LOAF
### (bacanie)

---

¾ cup / 200 g. unsalted butter
¾ cup / 200 ml. confectioners' sugar
6 eggs (separated)
1 tsp. baking powder
1 tbsp. vanilla extract
6 tbsp. flour
4 oz. / 100 g. peanuts (chopped)
4 oz. / 100 g. walnuts (chopped)
4 oz. / 100 g. almonds (chopped)
4 oz. / 100 g. Turkish delight (chopped)
4 oz. / 100 g. raisins (chopped)
4 oz. / 100 g. figs (chopped)
4 oz. / 100 g. candied orange peel

Beat the butter with the sugar. Add the egg yolks one by one. Now add the baking powder, vanilla, and flour and mix well. Add all the nuts, Turkish delight, and fruits and mix well. Beat the egg whites until stiff and fold into the mixture. Pour into a greased and floured loaf pan and bake at 350 degrees (180 degrees C) until a toothpick inserted in the center comes out dry, approximately 40 minutes. Allow to cool in the pan.

# MAZURKA
## (mazurcă)

The mazurka got is name from the dance. The dessert dates all the way back to the time of Chopin, when it was served at parties where music was played and mazurkas were danced. There are many variations, but here are two that my grandmother always made.

¾ cup / 200 ml. sugar
10 eggs (separated)
¾ cup / 200 ml. flour
¾ cup / 200 ml. raisins
¾ cup / 200 ml. golden raisins
¾ cup / 200 ml. chopped figs
Peel of 1 orange (minced)
1 tbsp. vanilla extract
¾ cup / 200 ml. ground almonds

Beat together the sugar and egg yolks, then add the flour, fruits, vanilla, and almonds. Beat the egg whites to stiff peaks and carefully fold into the mixture. Pour into a greased and parchment-paper-lined rectangular cake pan and bake at 350 degrees (180 degrees C) for 30-40 minutes.

# CHOCOLATE AND CREAM MAZURKA
## (mazurcă cu ciocolata şi frişcă)

Birthday parties are very exciting events for children—I could never sleep the night before mine. When I was a little girl, my mother always had my grandmother's help in preparing the sweets for my birthday party. There was always a chocolate and cream mazurka. There were also *cornuleţe*, little horns made of puff pastry and filled with cream or Turkish delight, as well as chocolate cream balls, rolled in powdered sugar and presented in pretty little cupcake holders.

As my birthday is in the spring, the table would always be set outside in the garden, with all the new blooms appearing. My friends were always very impressed with the variety of delights for them to sample and would be sent home with goodie bags containing more than their parents thought was necessary.

¾ cup / 200 g. sugar
8 egg yolks
4 tbsp. ground almonds
4 tbsp. shaved dark chocolate
5 tbsp. flour
2 egg whites (beaten stiff)
1⅔ cups / 400 g. whipped cream
Cocoa powder

Beat together the sugar and egg yolks. Add the almonds and chocolate and mix well. Add the flour bit by bit. Fold in the beaten egg whites. Pour into a greased and parchment-paper-lined rectangular cake pan and bake at 350 degrees (180 degrees C) for about 40 minutes. When ready and cooled, slice the cake into two layers and fill with whipped cream. Sprinkle the top of the cake with cocoa powder. Serve in square slices.

# WALNUT AND MARMALADE CAKE
## (prajitură cu nuci și marmeladă)

---

¾ cup / 200 ml. sugar
4 egg yolks
¾ cup / 200 ml. unsalted butter
¾ cup / 200 ml. sour cream
½ tsp. baking soda
1 tbsp. vanilla extract
2 cups / 500 g. flour
Marmalade (orange or apricot)
6 egg whites (beaten stiff)
¾ cup / 200 ml. confectioners' sugar
¾ cup / 200 g. ground walnuts

Beat together the sugar, egg yolks, and butter. Add the sour cream, baking soda, and vanilla and mix well. Now add the flour a little at a time until a soft dough is formed. Pour into a greased cake pan. Smooth flat, and cover with marmalade. To the beaten egg whites add the confectioners' sugar and walnuts, folding carefully. Pour this mixture over the marmalade in the cake pan. Bake at 350 degrees (180 degrees C) for 40 minutes or until cake pulls away from sides of pan.


# RASPBERRY CAKE
## (prajitură cu zmeură)

---

Raspberries are my mother's favorite fruit. Every time I see any when I am shopping I make sure to buy her some. They always bring her memories of the forest walks she took as a child with her parents in the summers in Romania. She would wander around the bushes looking for berries and gather as many as she could hold in her little hands, which were stained red by the time she managed to devour her collection.

1 cup / 250 g. ricotta cheese
2 hard-boiled egg yolks
3 eggs (separated)
2 tbsp. butter
1 tsp. salt
⅓ cup / 100 g. sugar
1 lb. / 500 g. fresh raspberries

Mix together the ricotta and all the egg yolks. Add the butter, salt, and sugar. Beat everything together to get a smooth cream. Beat the egg whites until stiff and fold into the cheese. Pour into a greased and floured cake pan and cover with the raspberries. Bake 30-40 minutes at 350 degrees (180 degrees C).

## MARBLE CAKE
### (marmor kuchen)

3 eggs (separated)
½ cup / 125 g. sugar
½ cup / 125 g. butter
½ cup / 125 g. flour
1 tsp. baking powder
½ cup / 125 ml. milk
1 tbsp. vanilla extract
2 tbsp. unsweetened cocoa powder

Beat the egg yolks, sugar, and butter until fluffy. Beat the whites until stiff. Fold the flour and egg yolks a bit at a time into the egg whites. Mix the baking powder into the milk. Add the vanilla to the milk. Mix into the cake dough. Pour half the mixture into a greased and floured loaf tin. To the other half, still in the bowl, add the cocoa powder. Pour in a swirling line over the center of the mixture in the pan (do not go to the edge). Bake about 1 hour at 350 degrees (180 degrees C). Allow to cool completely before removing from the pan.

# CREAM ROLL
## (ruladă cu frişcă)

**6 eggs (separated)**
**6 tbsp. confectioners' sugar**
**1 cup / 250 g. flour**
**3 tsp. cocoa powder**
**1⅓ cups / 350 g. whipped cream**
**Confectioners' sugar**

Beat together the egg yolks and 6 tbsp. sugar. Add the flour and cocoa powder. Beat the egg whites until stiff and fold into the mixture. Grease and line a deep cookie sheet with parchment paper. Pour the mixture on in a smooth thin layer. Bake about 30 minutes at 300 degrees (160 degrees C). Cool and turn onto a clean damp towel. Spread the whipped cream over the pastry. Fold one long end inwards and roll the pastry with the help of the towel. Serve sprinkled with confectioners' sugar.

# ROMANIAN BRIOCHE
## (cozonac)

The *cozonac* is a sweet bread associated with Easter in Romania. Along with the religious customs of the country at this time of year, the old tradition of giving Easter eggs, *pască* (an Easter cake), and *cozonac* to the poor is still observed today. There are several variations of this bread, but this is the classic recipe.

> 1½ cups / 375 ml. milk
> 2 tbsp. yeast
> 1 tsp. sugar (for the yeast)
> 4 cups / 1 kg. flour
> 8 eggs (separated)
> 2 tsp. salt
> 1 cup / 250 g. sugar
> 1 cup / 250 g. melted butter
> ½ cup / 125 g. raisins
> 1 egg yolk (beaten)

In a saucepan, warm up ½ cup milk. In a small bowl, mix it with the yeast and 1 tsp. sugar. In a saucepan, bring ½ cup milk to the boil, then pour it over 3 tbsp. flour. Beat to get rid of clumps. When this mixture has just cooled enough to touch, add it to the yeast and beat to fill the mixture with air bubbles. Sprinkle with a bit of flour and leave covered in a warm place for at least ½ hour. Beat the 8 egg yolks with salt until they darken in color. Add the sugar and beat to get a frothy mixture. Beat 4 of the egg whites stiff. In a warm bowl, pour the remaining flour and make a well in the center. Add the beaten egg yolks and slowly mix in the flour. Add the yeast mixture. Add 1 tbsp. warm milk and finally the egg whites. Using your hands, mix together all the remaining flour and knead the dough for 10 minutes. Place the dough on a floured surface and gradually add the melted butter, kneading until the dough is uniform and elastic, about ½ hour. Add a bit of warm milk if the dough becomes too dry. Add in the raisins, place in a bowl, and cover with a towel. Leave at least 1 hour for the dough to double in size.

Cut the dough in 3 and twist each piece to look like a long rope. Wrap each twisted piece in a greased round cake pan, one layer above the other. Brush with egg yolk and bake at 350 degrees (180 degrees C) for about 1 hour. Allow to cool 10 minutes before removing from the pan.

# ROMANIAN NUT BRIOCHE
## (cozonac cu nucă)

---

¾ cup / 190 ml. sugar
1 tbsp. vanilla extract
1 cup / 250 ml. warm milk
1 cup / 250 g. ground walnuts
2 tbsp. rum
**Romanian Brioche dough without raisins**

To make the filling, in a saucepan over medium-low heat, dissolve the sugar and vanilla in the milk. After about 5 minutes of simmering add the walnuts, stirring continuously so that they do not stick to the bottom of the saucepan. Simmer until it begins to thicken, 10-15 minutes. Remove from heat and add the rum. When the filling has cooled, roll out all the dough to ½ inch (1 cm.) thickness. Spread the filling over the dough, then roll the dough up tightly. In a greased round cake pan, wrap the roll into a circle. Allow to rise for ½ hour. Bake at 350 degrees (180 degrees C) for 45 minutes to 1 hour.

# Other Desserts

The landscapes of Romania, and the lives and struggles of its people, have been wonderfully depicted by two geniuses working in different media: the composer George Enescu (teacher of Yehudy Menuhin) and the painter Ion Grigorescu. The latter's paintings include colorful, vivid images of rural Romania, with its people at work and rest, and its magnificent scenery.

The music of Enescu became renowned worldwide. He is the composer of the famous "Romanian Rhapsody," a compilation of memorable tunes based on enchanting Romanian folk songs. The violin, *nai* (pan flute), and *ţambal* (cymbal) are typical Romanian instruments. Masterful musicians such as the famed Zamfir have made them well known.

The little pastries and sweets my grandmother used to make remind me of happy music because I always associate them with parties. Making trays laden with enough of these to satisfy all my hungry little friends was no easy task. Nevertheless, my proud grandmother was happiest when preparing desserts, even if she spent the whole day making them, and I think that her enthusiasm rubbed off on me.

These days the busy lives that most people lead do not allow them to spend time working on the presentation of small morsels of food that will be devoured within minutes, but in my grandmother's day it was her greatest joy to make cookies and little chocolate treats presented in the most professional fashion. Some of these can be found in this chapter.

# CHOCOLATE HAZELNUT CREAM
## (cremă de ciocolată cu alune pralinate)

***

5 tbsp. sugar
5 tbsp. hazelnuts
4 eggs
1 cup / 250 g. confectioners' sugar
1 cup / 250 g. unsalted butter
3 tbsp. cocoa powder
2 tbsp. milk

Heat the sugar in a pan over medium heat until it starts browning, about 5 minutes. Add the hazelnuts and cook for just a few minutes. Quickly turn the nuts out onto a greased plate. When cool break the nuts up roughly into small pieces. Place a bowl over a saucepan of simmering water over heat. Beat the eggs with the sugar in the bowl until they become creamy. Remove from heat and allow to cool. Add the butter cut into small pieces. Dissolve the cocoa powder in the milk and add to the eggs. Whip up the mixture. Mix in the hazelnuts. Spoon the cream into individual cups or Tartlet Shells (see below). Refrigerate until ready to serve. Decorate with ground nuts and confectioners' sugar, if desired.

# TARTLET SHELLS
## (tarte)

***

This is a useful recipe for individual tartlets that can be filled with any fruit, jelly, or cream dessert.

⅓ cup / 100 g. confectioners' sugar
1 cup / 250 g. unsalted butter
1 egg
1 tbsp. vanilla extract
2 cups / 500 g. flour

Beat together the sugar and butter, then add the egg and vanilla. Now add the flour and mix well. Knead into a smooth dough. Cut the dough into 6 equal pieces and roll each out on a floured surface. Place the rolled-out sheets in greased tartlet dishes, cutting away the excess dough. Prick the bases with a fork. Bake for 15-20 minutes at 325 degrees (170 degrees C). Carefully remove from the dishes and allow to cool.

# BURNT SUGAR CREAM
## (cremă de zahăr ars)

The old-fashioned way of making this cream was to cover the lid of the pan with hot coals as well as providing heat from below, but a double boiler works just as well. The result is something similar to the French crème caramel, although here the sugar isn't burned under the broiler but is prepared as the bottom of the cream before it is inverted to serve.

> 2⅓ cups / 600 ml. milk
> 1 vanilla pod
> 6 eggs
> ¾ cup / 200 g. sugar

In a saucepan, bring the milk and vanilla to the boil. Remove from heat, cover, and set aside. Next beat the eggs and 6 tbsp. sugar until the sugar appears to dissolve. Reheat the milk to boiling and remove the vanilla. Add the milk by spoonfuls to the eggs, beating, until the cream cools.

Place the remaining sugar in the top pan of a double boiler, or in a small saucepan that will fit into a larger pot. Heat the small pan directly over medium heat until the sugar starts to brown and melt. Remove from heat and swirl the pan around to coat the whole bottom in an even layer. Now add the cream and cover. Place this small pan in the bigger one. Fill the bigger pan with enough hot water to come halfway up the small pan. Simmer over medium-low heat, covered, for 25-30 minutes. The cream is ready when it pulls away from the pan walls easily. Remove from the water and allow to cool, then refrigerate the cream in the pan. When ready to serve, turn out onto a plate.

## RED WINE MOLD
### (jeleu de vin roşu)

---

**4 cups / 1 l. red wine**
**¾ cup / 200 g. sugar**
**¼ vanilla pod**
**10 sheets gelatin (soaked in a bowl of cold water)**

Bring the wine, sugar, and vanilla to the boil. Simmer on low heat for 10 minutes. Remove from heat and add the gelatin sheets (discard the water). When slightly cooled, strain the liquid and pour into a mold or individual cups. Refrigerate until set.

## CURRANT MOLD
### (jeleu de coacaze)

---

**1 lb. / 500 g. red currants**
**¾ cup / 200 ml. water**
**2 cups / 500 g. sugar**

Boil 1⅔ cups (400 g.) currants in the water and sugar. Simmer over medium heat until the fruit softens, about 20 minutes. Pour into a strainer and push the currants through, leaving the solids behind. Simmer the liquid over medium heat until thickened, about 10 minutes. Test this by spooning a few drops onto a cold plate. If they solidify after a few minutes, the sauce is ready. Otherwise, increase the time and test again. Then keep it warm.

Put a layer of some of the uncooked currants in the bottom of a mold. Pour some of the sauce over this layer. Place the mold in the freezer for several minutes. When set add another layer of currants and sauce and repeat the freezing. Continue to the top of the mold and refrigerate. When ready to serve, turn out onto a plate.

## COFFEE MOLD
### (jeleu de cafea)

Coffee is a much-loved drink in Romania. Thanks to the fact that the country was once part of the Ottoman Empire, Turkish coffee is a favorite. This may explain the popularity of this next dessert.

> 2 cups / 500 ml. milk
> ¼ vanilla pod
> 5 egg yolks
> 4 tbsp. confectioners' sugar
> 2 tbsp. coffee essence (see Othello Torte)
> 8 sheets gelatin (soaked in a bowl of cold water)

Simmer the milk and vanilla on medium heat for 10 minutes. Remove the vanilla. Cover the milk and set aside. Beat the egg yolks and sugar together, then slowly pour into the milk, beating continuously. Reheat uncovered on low and keep beating until it begins to thicken, about 10 minutes. Allow to cool slightly. Add the coffee and gelatin (discard the water). Mix well and pour into a mold or individual cups. Refrigerate until set.

# APPLE FOAM
## (spumă de mere)

1 lb. / 500 g. apples (peeled, seeded, and quartered)
2 cups / 500 ml. water
⅔ cup / 150 ml. sugar
3 sheets gelatin (soaked in a bowl of cold water)

Over medium heat, simmer the apple slices in the water until they soften, about 20 minutes. Drain and keep the cooking liquid in a saucepan. Mash the apples into a purée. Heat the apple juice over medium heat. Add the sugar and drained gelatin and simmer for 5 minutes. Allow to cool but not set. In a blender, blend the apple purée and juice until very fluffy. Quickly pour into cups and serve. Other fruits may be substituted.

# VANILLA NUT ROLLS
## (cornulețe de vanillie cu nuci)

⅔ cup / 150 g. unsalted butter
3 tbsp. sugar
3 tbsp. ground walnuts
1 vanilla pod
⅔ cup / 150 g. flour

Beat together the butter, sugar, and walnuts. Cut down the middle of the vanilla pod and with the tip of the knife scrape out the seeds. Beat the seeds into the butter mix. Mix in the flour until it forms a more solid dough. Take a piece of dough the size of a plum and roll it on a floured board into a 10-inch (25-cm.) stick the thickness of a finger. Cut the stick into 5 equal pieces. Roll each piece flat and shape into a hollow roll.

Repeat with the remaining dough. Place the rolls on a greased cookie sheet and bake for 15-20 minutes at 350 degrees (180 degrees C).

# CHOCOLATE SQUARES
## (fursecuri cu ciocolat )
ă

Childhood illnesses are unpleasant, and although it is a time when one often feels spoiled, it is also a hated time— who likes to recall having measles? My grandparents always had a miracle cure. Whenever I was a bit under the weather, my grandfather brought me one square of chocolate, which tasted divine. No matter what type of chocolate it was, he always called it *ours of the Dorna* (bear of the Dorna), after a beautiful mountain settlement in the northern Carpathian Mountains.

As I got older, my culinary tastes became more refined, but I have seldom tasted chocolate as sweet and soothing as Granddad's dark *ours*. Here is a recipe using dark chocolate that conjures up that taste.

> 1 cup / 250 g. confectioners' sugar
> ⅔ cup / 150 g. cup unsalted butter
> 1 egg white
> 1 tbsp. vanilla extract
> 1 cup / 250 g. ground hazelnuts
> 4 tbsp. flour

Mix the sugar and butter together. Add the egg white and beat until fluffy. Now add the vanilla, hazelnuts, and flour and blend well. Pour the mixture onto a greased and parchment-paper-lined cookie sheet, about ⅓ inch (1 cm.) thick. Bake 20-30 minutes at 325 degrees (170 degrees C).

⅔ cup / 150 g. chopped dark chocolate
1 tbsp. sugar
2 tbsp. water
1 tsp. rum extract

In a saucepan over low heat, melt the chocolate with the sugar and water. Stir while heating and add the rum. When the baked mixture is cooled, pour the warm chocolate onto it. Cut into squares, allow to cool, and serve.

## TRADITIONAL TEA BISCUITS
### (pesmiciori pentru ceai)

2 eggs
½ cup / 125 g. sugar
½ cup / 125 g. unsalted butter
⅓ cup / 100 g. flour
2 tsp. rum
4 oz. / 100 g. raisins

Beat together the eggs and sugar. Add the butter and mix well. Add the flour, rum, and raisins and mix again. Grease and flour a cookie sheet. Using a spoon dipped in hot water, take spoonfuls of batter and place on the sheet in almond shapes. Leave about ⅔ inch (1½ cm.) between the biscuits. Bake at 350 degrees (180 degrees C) for 15-20 minutes. Traditionally these biscuits are served with the afternoon tea.

# CUMIN AND NUT BISCUITS
## (pişcoturi cu chimen şi nuci)

2 eggs
½ cup / 125 g. sugar
1 tsp. butter
20 walnuts (cleaned and ground)
1 tsp. baking soda
1 tsp. ground cumin
1 cup / 250 g. flour

Mix the eggs and sugar. Add the butter, nuts, baking soda, cumin, and flour. Beat well. On a floured board, roll out 2 square sheets ¾ inch (2 cm.) thick. Place on greased cookie sheets and bake 20-30 minutes at 350 degrees (180 degrees C). When still warm, cut into long thin sticks, like biscotti.

# ANISEED BISCUITS
## (pesmeţi cu anason)

3 tbsp. yeast
¾ cup / 190 g. sugar
2 cups / 500 ml. milk (warm)
2 cups / 500 g. flour
½ tsp. salt
2 whole eggs
1 tbsp. vanilla extract
½ cup / 125 g. melted butter
1 egg yolk (beaten)
1 tsp. ground aniseed
3 tbsp. confectioners' sugar

In a bowl, mix the yeast with 1 tsp. sugar. Add ½ cup (125

ml.) milk and enough flour to make a porridgelike mixture. Leave to rise until the volume doubles, about 1 hour. Add the remaining milk, sugar, salt, eggs, vanilla, and butter. Knead well until it begins forming bubbles. Split the dough into 2 and place each piece in separate rectangular cake pans. Cover and put in a warm place for 1 hour until the doughs rise and the cake pans look full. Brush with egg yolk and bake at 350 degrees (180 degrees C) for 40-50 minutes. After 2-3 days, cut the cakes into thin slices like biscotti, place the slices on a cookie sheet, and bake for 30 minutes at 350 degrees (180 degrees C) until they are dry. Allow to cool. Mix the aniseed and confectioners' sugar. Sprinkle on the slices. Serve cold.

# SESAME COOKIES
## (covrigei cu susan)

---

3 tbsp. confectioners' sugar
⅔ cup / 150 g. unsalted butter
1 egg (separated)
2 tbsp. milk
1 tsp. baking powder
1 tsp. vanilla extract
1 cup / 250 g. flour
2 tbsp. sesame seeds

Beat together the sugar, butter, and egg yolk. Add the milk, baking powder, and vanilla and mix well. Next add the flour and mix. Refrigerate for 20-30 minutes. Take tablespoonfuls and, using damp hands, shape balls into flat cookies on a greased cookie sheet. Brush the cookies with egg white and sprinkle with sesame seeds. Bake 15-20 minutes at 325 degrees (170 degrees C).

# COFFEE TRUFFLES
## (trufe de cafea)

1 cup / 250 g. sugar
1 cup / 250 g. unsalted butter
1 egg yolk
2 tbsp. coffee essence (see Othello Torte)
3 hard-boiled egg yolks (crumbled)
Cocoa powder

Beat together the sugar, butter, and raw egg yolk. Add the coffee essence and crumbled egg yolks. Mix everything well until very smooth. Using moist hands, roll teaspoonfuls of the mixture into ball shapes, then roll them through cocoa powder. Refrigerate and serve cold.

# CHOCOLATE POTATOES
## (cartofi)

1 cup / 250 ml. milk
⅓ cup / 100 ml. sugar
1 vanilla pod
5 tbsp. chopped walnuts
2 tbsp. rum
4 tbsp. cocoa powder
1⅓ cups / 400 ml. ground almonds
Cocoa powder or confectioners' sugar

Heat the milk and sugar over low heat for 10 minutes. Cut the vanilla pod down the middle, scrape out the seeds, and add the seeds to the milk. Add the walnuts, rum, and cocoa powder. Simmer for about 10 minutes over medium heat, then add the almonds. Combine all the ingredients well and remove from heat. When the mixture is cool enough to handle, take tablespoonfuls and form into small potato shapes. Roll through a plate of cocoa powder or confectioners' sugar. Refrigerate until ready to serve. This can be made several days in advance.

## FRIED CHEESE TRIANGLES
### (placintele prajite cu brînză)

3 tbsp. oil
¾ cup / 200 ml. water
2 tsp. salt
1-2 cups / 250-500 g. flour
2 tbsp. melted butter
1⅓ cups / 400 g. ricotta cheese
3 eggs
1 tsp. ground cinnamon
2 tbsp. sugar
1 egg (beaten)
Confectioners' sugar

Mix together the oil, water, 1 tsp. salt, and enough flour to form a soft dough. Cover with a towel and leave for 15 minutes. Roll out the dough on a floured board to form a rectangle of ½-inch (1-cm.) thickness. Brush the dough with half the butter, then fold the sheet in thirds (like when covering a parcel). Refrigerate 10 minutes. Roll out the dough again and repeat the buttering, folding, and refrigerating.

Meanwhile make the filling by mixing together the cheese, 3 eggs, cinnamon, sugar, and remaining salt. Roll out the dough once more, but this time cut it into squares of about 6 inches (15 cm.). Place a spoonful of the cheese mixture in the center of each dough square, brush the edges with beaten egg, and fold into a triangle. Melt more butter in a pan and, over high heat, fry the triangles about 3 minutes per side until golden. When cooled, sprinkle with confectioners' sugar.

# BUTTER BALLS
## (corăbioare)

¾ cup / 190 g. butter
1 cup / 250 g. confectioners' sugar
1 tbsp. vanilla extract
3 tbsp. yeast
1 tsp. salt
½ cup / 125 ml. milk
2 cups / 500 g. flour

In a bowl, mix together the butter, 1 tbsp. sugar, and the vanilla. Dissolve the yeast and salt in the milk. Add to the mixture. Add flour until a relatively firm dough is formed (you may need more or less than stated). Leave in the bowl to rise for 1 hour. Next divide the dough into 3 parts. Roll each piece into a long stick ⅔ inch (1.5 cm.) thick, then cut into pieces ¾ inch (2 cm.) long. Place the pieces on a greased cookie sheet and leave for 30 minutes to rise again. Bake for 20-30 minutes at 350 degrees (180 degrees C). When still warm, roll in the remaining sugar.

# DELICIOUS LIES
## (minciuni delicioase)

2 cups / 500 g. flour
3 egg yolks
1 whole egg
2 tbsp. sour cream
2 tbsp. carbonated mineral water
1 tsp. rum extract
1 tsp. confectioners' sugar
1 tsp. salt
2 tbsp. butter
Confectioners' sugar for coating

On a wooden board, make a mound out of the flour, then make a well in its center. Place the eggs, sour cream, water, rum, sugar, and salt in the well. Slowly work the flour into the center of the well until a firm dough is formed (add flour if necessary). Split the dough into two and leave to rest 1 hour. Now roll out the dough on a floured board until it is as thin as possible. Cut into strips about 1¼ inches (4 cm.) wide, and cut these into pieces 3 inches (10 cm.) long. Take each piece and make a small cut ⅓ from an end, then work the other end through the hole to make the piece look like a knot. Fry in butter over high heat until golden brown, about 5 minutes. Drain on paper towels. Sprinkle with lots of confectioners' sugar.

## CAT'S TONGUES
### (limbi de pisică)

---

¾ cup / 180 g. butter
1 cup / 250 g. sugar
1 cup / 250 g. flour
1 tsp. vanilla extract
7 egg whites

Melt the butter and mix with the sugar. When the mixture becomes creamy, add the flour and vanilla. Beat the egg whites until stiff and fold into the mixture. Line a cookie sheet with greased parchment paper and, using a spoon, place stick shapes of the mixture onto the sheet. Bake at 325 degrees (170 degrees C) for about 15 minutes, until the edges begin to brown lightly. Remove from the cookie sheet while still warm; otherwise they will break. Allow to cool. Serve with coffee or next to ice cream.

# CHERRY COMPOTE
## (compot de cireşe)

Fruit compotes may be served with cakes, ice cream, or on their own.

**2 lb. / 1 kg. cherries with pits**
**3 tbsp. sugar**
**1 vanilla pod**
**Water to cover**

In a pot, place the cherries, sugar, vanilla, and water. Bring to the boil, then lower the heat to medium and simmer for about 1 hour, until the cherries are soft and syrupy. Remove the vanilla. Serve compote cold.

# APPLE COMPOTE
## (compot de mere)

**6 large crisp apples**
**2⅓ cups / 600 ml. water**
**1 cup / 250 g. sugar**
**1 cinnamon stick**
**3 cloves**
**1 lemon (halved)**
**6 prunes (pitted)**

Peel the apples, remove the seeds, and cut into four. Drop the slices into a bowl of cold water. Bring 2⅓ cups water, the sugar, cinnamon, and cloves to the boil. Add the drained apples, the lemon, and prunes. Cover and simmer over low heat until the apples soften and the water has turned into a fragrant syrup. This will take about 30-40 minutes. Remove the cinnamon and lemon. Serve compote cold.

# ROSE JAM
## (dulceață de trandafir)

My grandparents' garden was a magical place. The foliage of the huge trees provided shade, and the multicolored flowers sent out intoxicating frangrances. It was a perfect place for a child to play. Indeed, this is where my brothers and I had the best times of our childhood—climbing, running, sampling unripe plums and apples.

One of my favorite corners was the rose border. I was fascinated by the flowers' silky petals, warm colors, and unforgettable perfume. Great was my surprise when one day my grandmother invited me to help her pick the petals off a particular variety in the garden. This was in order to make a magical preserve. I can still smell the aroma of the rose petals simmering with sugar to make a delicious jam with a very unique taste. Even today, when a guest enters a house in Romania, he is often offered a spoonful of rose jam accompanied by a glass of ice-cold water. There is nothing more refreshing on a hot summer day.

> **1 cup / 250 g. rose petals (see below)**
> **1 tsp. salt**
> **4 cups / 1 l. water**
> **Juice of ½ lemon**
> **5 cups / 1¼ kg. sugar**

Choose petals of open roses, of a fragrant variety. Separate the petals into 2 groups, the prettier petals and the less perfect ones (the weights should be equal). Place the nicer bunch of petals in bowl and rub the salt vigorously into them, then refrigerate for 2 hours. Meanwhile, boil the other petals in the water for 4 minutes. Cool and add the lemon juice. When the liquid is cold, pass it though a fine sieve.

In a heavy saucepan, mix the sugar and 3 cups of the liquid.

Simmer over low heat until the sugar dissolves completely, about 10 minutes. Add the refrigerated petals and simmer over medium heat for 15-25 minutes until the liquid thickens, removing any foam that forms as it simmers. The liquid should coat the back of a spoon and solidify. Once the liquid is ready, transfer to glass jars, cover, and leave for at least 12 hours. Serve the jam with white bread, or on its own on a spoon to accompany coffee.

# Index

fried courgettes in sour cream,
125
fried liver, 113
fried pepper salad, 44
fruit and nut loaf, 170

## G

garlic soup, 62
goulash, 100
green been borscht, 64
green beans with egg and
cheese, 126
green bell peppers, 20, 102
green corn soup, 60
grilled mackerels with hot
sauce, 83
grilled pepper salad, 43

## H

herring and nut spread, 39
herring and onion salad, 49
Hungarian potatoes, 122

## K

kidneys in white-wine sauce,
112

## L

lamb, 26, 108, 110
lamb chorba, 68
leek and bean salad, 47

leeks with olives, 129
lentil soup, 61
loaf, 169, 170

## M

mămăligă, 132, 133
macaroni and tomato sauce
budincă, 142
mackerel, 82, 83
marble cake, 174
marinated cabbage, 120
marinated carp, 75
marinated meatballs, 109
marinated olives, 37
mashed butter beans, 127
mazurka, 171
meat and green bean stew,
104
meat budincă, 143
meringue cream torte, 156
mititei, 106
mocha torte, 164
mold, 183, 184
Moldavian borscht, 66
Moldavian hamburgers, 108
monastic stew, 118
mosaic bread, 23
Muresh-style goulash, 100
mushroom and fish
croquettes, 28
mushroom budincă, 141
mushroom gelatin with
mayonnaise, 29
mushroom pilaf, 130

# N

Napoleon torte, 166

# O

olives, 37, 111, 129
Othello torte, 159

# P

partridge pilaf, 98
peas on fried bread, 35
peasant chicken chorba, 69
peasant-style courgettes, 126
peppers, 18, 43, 44, 134, 135
peppers pickled in vinegar, 134
perch, 77, 79
pickled carp, 77
pickled stuffed peppers, 135
pike, 81
poached mayonnaise perch, 79
Polish cauliflower, 131
Polish veal stew, 101
Polish-style perch, 77
potato and carrot roll, 124
potato and cheese budincă, 139
potato salad, 46
potato stew, 122
potatoes, 47
provolone, 35, 85

# R

radish salad, 48
raspberry cake, 173
red and white cabbage salad, 48
red wine mold, 183
rice and wine budincă, 148
roast duckling on sweet cabbage, 96
roast duckling with baked apples, 97
roe, 50
Romanian beef stew, 104
Romanian brioche, 176
Romanian fried carp, 73
Romanian kebabs, 106
Romanian meatloaf, 107
Romanian nut brioche, 177
Romanian soup noodles, 70
rose jam, 195
Russian chorba, 67
Russian loaf, 169
Russian salad, 47
Russian-style aubergines, 128
Russian-style trout, 87

# S

salad à la Prague, 51
salami, 27, 51, 146
salami budincă, 146
salami croquettes, 27
sauerkraut-stuffed potato cakes, 124

savory fried cheese patties, 34
semolina budincă, 149
semolina croquettes, 131
sesame cookies, 189
skate in red wine, 80
small pickles, 136
soufflé, 168
sour cream budincă, 146
sour cream soufflé, 168
spinach pancake budincă, 140
squares, 187
stuffed baked grape leaves, 26
stuffed baked pike, 81
stuffed peppers, 102
stuffed red peppers, 129
stuffed white cabbage, 103
sturgeon, 85, 86
summer-fruit charlotte, 168
sweet cheese budincă, 152
sweet cornmeal budincă, 150

T

tartar sauce, 27
Timishoara-style spread, 38
toast with Roquefort butter or black butter, 37
tomato soup, 57
tomatoes, 18, 19, 57, 87
tongue salad, 52
tongue with olives, 111

torte, 157, 158, 160, 161, 163, 164, 165
traditional borscht, 63
traditional tea biscuits, 187
trout, 87

U

Ukranian borscht, 65
urdă, 38

V

vanilla nut rolls, 185
veal, 65, 99, 100, 101, 102, 103, 143
vegetable and apple salad, 49
vegetable ratatouille, 117
vegetable soup with sour cream, 55
vegetable-stuffed bread cups, 24

W

walnut and marmalade cake, 173
walnut budincă, 147
whey cheese with dill, 38
wine sauce, 147

Z

zucchini, 46